VIOLETS
in the
SNOW

GARY & KIM ELLIOT

FOLLOWING GOD INTO THE ROMANTIC
THE EXTRAORDINARY LOVE STORY OF THE ELLIOT'S

GRP
God of the Romantique Publications

Violets in the Snow

Published in Nashville, Tennessee, by God of the Romanitque Publications.

Special discounts are available on quantity purchases by corporations, associations, and others. Orders by US trade bookstores and wholesalers—for details, contact the publisher at grpnashville@gmail.com

ISBN: 9798880188307

First Edition: 2024

This love story, our love story, is dedicated to our grandkids
or my "Bugg'rs", as I like to call them…
If Pops and I can leave you anything of true worth this side of Heaven,
it will be a legacy of daring faith in…
God's personal love for you
His holy purposes for you and
His great desire to be the One to give you the gift of
a priceless mate to marry
He gives the best gifts, and He will always be worth your wait
We know this is the truth first from His word
and now from our experiences of being given the gifts of
one another, of your parents, and of you!

Love Always & Forever, Pops & GiGi

TABLE OF CONTENTS

INTRODUCTION

YESTERDAY, I (KIM) SAT ON our front steps after deadheading our knock-out rose bushes. Deadheading is a pruning practice where you cut off the head of a flower whose bloom is fading. It helps conserve the plant's energy from trying to save the spent flower and redirects it to make new flowers instead. Deadheading is a weekly chore Gary keeps for me to do because I enjoy the contemplation time it provides. When I finished, I started to ponder with Jesus how far we've come and how far we've yet to go. You see, where Gary and I are going with Jesus next is just as impossible for us to achieve as it has been for us to get as far as we have imagined up to this point, and I told Jesus with a hint of tone, "You know, I only asked for a husband. Gary only asked for a wife. Neither of us asked You to make a big deal of it." Be warned, friends; He *will* give you more than you could ever ask or imagine if you dare to believe Him for the impossible.

Have you ever met someone with decades of unspent romantic love? Someone who is waiting for "the one"? That was us. From early on, Gary and I could never shake the inner convictions of destiny and God's fatherly care to bring us the desire of our hearts in a spouse. We knew there had to be a better way than what the world *and* the Church offered us.

In November of 2022, I had a revelation: in my Spirit, I saw Father God strolling through The Garden of Beginnings. He was experiencing a grief of sorts. His eyes were drawn away deep in thought. His feet shuffled over the ever-fresh grasses of His Garden when He approached something seemingly out of order. Looking down, He was struck with curiosity, spotting something embedded in the dirt under His feet. Something soiled and distressed. He bent down, pushing centuries of sediment away from its nested edges. Delicately He pried it from its apparent grave and sees it's an invitation. It was an invitation He had handed over to His kids in the beginning. An invitation that by all indications had been dropped and long forgotten. I saw Him brush off the dirt, and bend back the worn corners in an attempt to smooth the creases out. He opens it. The invitation read, "Come, and I WILL make for you a suitable helper."

This was an invite Gary and I accepted as young adults. Gary, after several romantically broken hearts. And myself, after one tragically life-altering violation. The romantic redemption story planned for us is of Biblical proportions.

Let us increase your relentless hopes for your divine love story by telling you our love story. It is a love story that traces God's fingerprints throughout our childhood and young adulthood where God won our hearts and convinced us He was a provider of the best gift; a spouse fit to us and our purposes. We will pull back the curtains on the emotional roads we walked as singles to get through the narrow gates of promise. Much like an iceberg, it's all about developing the depths in order to support its heights.

Living on the opposite ends of our hometown, unknown to one another, we walked with Jesus into a mystery of deep intimacy and faith in Christ and eventually right into one another.

Here it is, Violets in the Snow, just one of the many things we never asked Him for nor imagined He would give us: a love story designed by Him to bless us beyond measure and be used to pivot the moral compass of an entire generation because He said so.

May you come to love the One who wrote it more than you've dared to ask or imagined could be possible. May you come to experience the worth of His perfect companionship with just you. May you come to experience not only why you live but why you wait for "the one" only He desires to give.

He is why we write. He is why we teach. He is why we entertain. He is why we love. He is why we live.

ACT 1

WHERE HAVE YOU BEEN ALL MY LIFE?

SCENE ONE:

NOT ALL THAT GLOWS IS NEON

- G -

Electric Art

FRIDAYS. FOR THIS SEVEN-YEAR-old, they were the highlight of my entire week. My father had received his pay just as he did at the end of every work week. As was our family ritual, we were out on the town every Friday night. Early in the night, we would be shopping, which thrilled my mother's heart. Later in the evening would be bowling league time, which thrilled my dad's heart. However, right now it was time for burgers and fries, fast-food style. This is what thrilled my little heart. This was the highlight of my highlight! Eating out in the city was a big deal to a tiny lad like myself. It wasn't merely peeling back the wrapping from a steamy burger and dipping salty fries; it was also the anticipation of a more fantastic experience, and like any other Friday, I couldn't wait.

When Dad made the sweeping right turn on that familiar busy street, I'd perk up from the back seat of our vinyl-topped coupe. That's where my favorite burger joint would first come into view. But it was glowing even more spectacularly on this particular evening due to the recent snowfall. The blanket of white vividly reflected a blinking wash of orange and blue radiating from the towering sign next to the eatery.

Even though it was late January, we elected to eat inside the car that night. I remember being sort of quiet, and my parents wondered why. My gaze out the side window had me occupied. My strawberry milkshake went down smoothly like the electric art of the radiant sign. It was almost like a miniature Vegas, and it had this seven-year-old thoroughly entertained.

Friday nights at the Burger spot were only one of my glowing fascinations. On the North side of town sat an old-school shopping center we frequented weekly with Mom. There was a larger department store that sold anything and everything, along with a market, barbershop, and an ice cream shop offering what seemed to be about a thousand flavors! That was all great, but I was interested in what was next to the entrance: a wonderful sign with giant colored balls and atomic stars that lit up like dozens of Christmas trees. Everything blinked off and on like all the features were dancing just for me. To my adolescent eyes, it was mesmerizing.

Next were the taverns. My father loved his beer and his bowling league. Strangely, I loved his beer, too but not for the reasons many would think. Hang with me. Despite his affection for his choice of suds, I do not recall ever seeing him in a blitzed state in front of me while growing up. He usually reserved his beverage consumption for the weekends only. That being said, there were many other occasions I would be tagging along when he darted into a local bar for a brew or two. As we entered the bar, I was fed all the nuts, popcorn, and Coke I wanted. Then, on top of that, I was given a handful of quarters to thrill me with pinball and other amusements while my dad and uncle (who often consumed with my father) tilted a few frosty ones. This was a regular part of my childhood. All that aside, do you know what I liked most about my adolescent tavern runs? Not the beer, of course, but it was the beer signs. Those bold advertisements lit up the sidewalks and city streets in an explosion of colors! I couldn't get enough! With my fascination with PBR, Old Style, and Stag glowing in my eyes at such a young age, it's a miracle you don't find me sloshed on the streets this weekend.

Do you see a common fascination here? The connecting factor? Neon. There is just something about neon lights that still enchants me today. What feels like a lifetime ago, as a knee-high lad, the most exciting places of business were the ones that did street advertising with these twisted gas-filled tubes in rainbow colors. They were dynamic, elegant, and just plain sexy! These days, neon isn't so prevalent. Newer technology has delivered more cost-effective alternatives to illuminate our city streets, so neon's glowing glory is reserved mainly for tourist destinations willing to invest in this more expensive expression of electric art. If you ask me, it's worth every dollar.

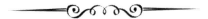

I had to shake myself to believe this was happening. How did we get here? So many years had passed as I continued to believe for the impossible that God Himself would send the one lady He had destined me to marry. This certainly took much longer than I had ever expected; decades went by, and I had survived all the struggles, questions, and tests. Honestly, it looked as if nothing would ever happen for me, but by sheer grace from the Heavens, I didn't give up on God granting this gift. He did not disappoint.

And now here we are. My new wife, Kim, and I are on our honeymoon, standing in the center of a street engulfed in a sea of captivating neon; what a sight! I felt like that elated seven-year-old boy all over again. Yes, it was happening. And this neon fascination was a reoccurring thing for both of us as of late. We had been preparing to relocate from our home in Illinois to the music city of Nashville. Several earlier journeys down south, in preparation for such a move, found us in the flash and country twang of lower Broadway Street, which is nothing but noise dressed in neon beauty. Tonight, however, it was New Orleans's famed Bourbon's turn to glow on us.

Our wedding just happened in late November of 2017. After our "I do's," we wasted no time. As early as the next morning, we loaded the red Chevy and hit the highway for New Orleans, where we would spend the week in the Louisiana autum sun. To our surprise, our hotel stood directly on the corner of the Bourbon Street buzz, another haven of exploding color all in neon.

Do you know how quickly time goes by when life is a sheer blast? It seemed like my bride, and I had just gotten to the Big Easy when it came time to trek back to the frozen Midwest. Yuk! So, after packing back up, we hit the highway once again. Our halfway point back home was Memphis, Tennessee, where we stopped to lodge our last night. But first, it was time to play just one more time. I guess we didn't get enough of it in New Orleans.

There we were, standing in yet another street immersed in neon. This time, it was the world-famous Beale Street in Memphis. I'll never forget the experience of slowly strolling through all that color at night, holding my girl's hand. It was a calm evening with a brisk chill. You could see our breath in the late Autumn Tennessee air. We were in a hurry for nothing.

My new bride and I had explored all the Memphis frolicking that we could handle in the Beale nightlife. We had watched some of the last street performers for the night and entered an antique soda shop filled with replicas of antique toys, among other gifts. The picture of a banana split behind the soda bar reminded me that we hadn't had our late meal yet. I knew both of us had most likely found a few additional pounds during the last week. We had devoured some killer eats and a lot of them. That being said, neither of us was in much of a mood for another heavy spread.

We looked up and down Beale, all lit up under fancy neon signs, for an eatery. For some odd reason, nothing stood out to us. For what felt like 30 minutes, we looked as if nothing was right for the moment. Strange. The searching commenced. Neither Kim nor I were prepared for what was about to happen. A million years of mere human striving would never be enough to plan such an experience. My girl and I were being drawn as if invited into something mind-blowing, and we didn't even have a clue!

I looked across the Beale; quietly tucked away between two massive bars was a little restaurant and music venue. The strange thing about it was that it had a very modest neon sign that seemed hidden from all the explosive signs around it. Just a red and white striped canopied cafe-styled joint; nothing was screaming, "Look at me! Eat here!" Since other options weren't fitting our mood, I pointed across the street and suggested, "What about that place?"

- K -
Electric Shock!

Cleaning up the dishes after dinner, news broke across the nation's airways—the king of rock and roll was dead. Elvis Presley died unexpectedly in his home, and I was sad, really sad, like he was a friend. I was 11 years old, living in east central Iowa and far from Memphis, Tennessee, and far from being a friend to Elvis Presley.

My parents were fans, but my mom was the biggest fan. We had a mid-century modern stereo console in our dining room. Our dining table was centered in the room with four chairs, leaving plenty of space between the stereo and surrounding chairs to roller skate across the century-old hardwood floor. I was infatuated with celebrity singers. I wanted to be one! I would sneak up to my parent's bedroom on weeknights, watch all the variety shows like Carol Burnett, Donny & Marie, and Sonny & Cher, and grab my mom's hair brush to sing along. I'd even practice Cher's signature lanky move of throwing that one string of hair back off from her dewy complexion.

Being a latch-key kid in the 80s, I'd get home from school, and with no parents in the house, I'd strap on my roller skates. I'd load up my favorite Elvis vinyl records and skate my legs off while singing my heart out. This did not make me my brother's favorite sister; unfortunately for him, I was his only sister. I loved Elvis! One of my favorite albums was his live recording, Elvis in Concert, which included live fan comments.

All that my parents loved about him as an artist and as a person was echoed in there. It was an immersive experience every time. That album came out in October following his death.

This year, his daughter, Lisa Marie, passed at age 54 from cardiac arrest. I couldn't stop watching and reading all the information filling my social media newsfeeds. I was sad again, like when her dad passed. But this time, I couldn't shake it, which was weird because I'm an adult fully aware of the brevity of life, and Lisa and I weren't friends any more than Elvis and I. They both captivated me the first time I saw that famous family shoot of Lisa Marie in her red, white, and blue polka-dot dress, catching her father's deep adorations and strangely tying my heart to Memphis, TN.

Beale, Broadway, Bourbon, and back to Beale. A proverbial full circle was about to complete in my life that last night honeymooning in Memphis. We'd come a long way, me and Jesus. That last night in Memphis had a sweet, slow roll to it as my brand-new husband and I, hand in hand, strolled Beale Street in a hurry for nothing, just like he said. Gary was not only my brand-new husband but my only husband. Gary was the one I had been waiting decades for. Our first week as husband and wife was spent alone, simply enjoying one another in random new places. New Orleans was a first-time visit for both of us. I remember two months into our engagement, thinking about where to honeymoon. I love the Rockies. My parents honeymooned there, and we made some family trips there growing up. Mountains take my breath away, and Gary had never been. The Rockies was my first thought, so I laid it on the table for Gary to consider.

However, over the next couple of days, in the back of my mind, a different destination kept coming and interrupting my thoughts. While we were having dinner at a great barbecue joint at the north end of our hometown, our conversation came around to the Rocky Mountain honeymoon I first suggested. I could tell Gary was not yet convinced it was something he wanted to do, so I laid out the other destination that had been nagging at me all week: Memphis, Tennessee. At first mention, his eyes raised with much more interest as he replied, "Hmm, like a full circle thing, huh?" He added New Orleans to our itinerary, and everything fit seamlessly into a delightful plan neither of us had seen before. It was going to be perfect!

I found the coolest high-end hotel at a cheap rate. The off-season is the way to go. When I booked our room, I had no idea it was on the corner of Bourbon Street. The glamorous lobby, fine cuisine breakfasts, high vaulted ceilings, and exposed brick walls of our room screamed urban chic, which heightened our delight. Our room had the tallest windows I had ever seen, and they overlooked all the neon excitement lighting up the city's heart. The only thing better than our digs was being together with nothing on the agenda but enjoying the joy of each other and the wonder of how God brought us together.

Memphis bookended our honeymoon. We started toward NOLA and had a quick first night in Memphis. We spoiled ourselves with a high-end hotel all about Elvis. On our way back from New Orleans, we planned to throw caution to the wind and grab a roadside dive. The last night of our honeymoon was super sweet. Neither of us was in a hurry to close this honeymoon down.

I was enjoying "learning" Gary. When I ask him questions about himself, he frequently wants to know why I am asking, and I'll tease, "I'm just learning you." Perusing through that soda polar, I would watch him pick up the circus-like wind-up toys with a far-away fondness blushing on his face, and he would tell me about times when he was a kid playing with such delicate treasures as these. I learned about his passion for quality craftsmanship from long ago. Knowing he said he was hungry for a "little something," I interrupted his browsing by suggesting a little ice cream from the soda counter. He looked at me, puzzled, as though I did not understand what "a little something" meant. I thought, "Okay, Kim, when your husband says he's hungry for a "little something," your dude is actually hungry for a meal, not a snack." Note taken.

As Gary and I exited the soda shop and stood outside its doors, peering through Beale's glitzy glow, surveying all the dining options vying for our bid that night, I felt strangely contemplative. I had often wondered if I'd ever find myself here again. I was no longer the same person, and it seemed like Memphis was no longer the same city. Looming in the fluorescent haze was a new irony: the last time I was on

Beale Street, my best friend and I were having a heavy discussion about my love life, or should I say, my lack of one. She suggested that my self-loathing kept me from being available to guys. I rebutted; I could not settle for anyone I could get for myself. I was a believer in fate, a love destined just for me. Boy, oh, boy, did God do a number on me. There was a love destined for me, all right. I was holding his hand tonight on Beale Street, but fate had nothing to do with it.

So many things had been made new in my life since then, and "what was" didn't seem to matter anymore. I stood on Beale Street, knowing fate never had its chance to define my future. Tonight, I felt the refreshing freedom of being made new and blessed beyond measure. It was promised, and it was a long time coming, but it was happening.

Gary, suggesting the joint directly across the street, asked me what I thought. I said, "That's fine, whatever you want." He replied, wanting to know what I preferred. I am so not used to my preferences being someone else's preference. I used to giggle when learning how to love and honor others; how are any decisions ever made when two selfless people only want to serve what the other prefers? Now, I find myself married to a man who wants to ensure my preferences are served first. Our desire to out-honor and out-serve the other often catches us up in indecision. With neither of us having any objections, we moved onto the red and white striped canopied cafe-styled joint directly across from us.

We walked past the abandoned hostess stand and through the double doors into a cozy haunt of what felt like an early speakeasy. A waitress invites us to take a seat wherever we please. It was late on a Monday, and only a few other couples were dining that night. Wooden square tables, set for four, were dressed with cloth napkin-wrapped silverware. We found ourselves wandering over to the more secluded corner of the room. Seclusion is always a natural appeal for honeymooners and introverts, which we both are.

I was so looking forward to this dinner and soaking up the last bit of togetherness with my husband as a crowning event to our honeymoon. However, I was becoming increasingly distracted inwardly as we took our seats. My eyes were taking in the dark wooden double doors, the dim lighting, and the towering heavy wooden bar backing the quaint dining area. The New Orleans ornate tin ceiling and wall sconces, slanting wooden floors, red velvet drapes, and red velour-papered walls. All that made up the atmosphere of this place built up into a spin of familiarity I could not quite nail down. Then, as I took my menu in hand, I heard the faint bellows of a blues guitarist. I casually glanced to the right, and I saw it. I saw that unforgettable sunken dining room fronting the small stage. Like an electric shock, a torrent of EVERYTHING came at me hard. It came at me fast. This is it! I can't believe it. THIS IS IT!

A waitress approached our table, asking for our orders. I stepped out of my mind-riot just long enough to order the first thing I saw on my menu. My interiors started quivering over where Gary and I had just landed. I was paralyzed in my thoughts. Do I tell him now or later? I was just "learning" him, after all. I couldn't keep this to myself; he was my husband and best friend. He'd hate knowing I sat through our entire dinner alone in this experience before disclosing to him where we had landed, right? Oh man, I hated to kill the romance, but I knew I had to tell him.

Gently, I put my hand on his forearm and leaned into him. Drawing his attention, I quietly said, "Gary, this is it. This is *that* place. My eyes pressed his to remember back to 26 years ago with me.

His eyes showed me that his mind was now spinning like mine. He was trying to catch his thoughts on what I had just announced. His puzzlement suddenly became full awareness as he confirmed, "This is *that* place?" I nodded in affirmation, still not knowing how to respond to this unbelievable event, when he put his arm firmly around my shoulders, drew me in close, and started to pray...

SCENE TWO:

THE "LOVE" ALL AROUND US

- G -

Skyscrapers, Lincoln, and Dirt

RAYS OF SUN EXPLODED INTO our hotel room. The warmth New Orleans shared with us was not to be taken for granted. Next week, we would be back home adjusting to this married thing as another Illinois winter would soon be roaring in. Burr! As for now, it was time to soak in all the southern spring-like weather we could. Kim was in the shower, and that wouldn't take too long, but next would come the make-up routine, and that was another story. So I just enjoyed the next moments alone. By the way, as a new husband, no one prepared me for the mountain of skincare and make-up provisions women collect. I confessed to Jesus, "This wife You have given me owns more make-up than all the boys in Kiss combined, and throw in Alice Cooper for good measure. Ugh, someone pray for me!"

Watching the buzz of traffic below our hotel, I told Jesus how thankful I was that He was true to do just as He said He would. God had promised me the right wife from His hand years ago. And here we were, on our honeymoon, skin care products and all. So how did it all happen? How did we get here? Read on; it's quite a tale.

Skyscrapers, Lincoln, and some of the richest dirt in the entire world make up the state of Illinois, our home state. That rich black soil is perfect for growing acres after endless acres of corn. It's not so good for butter and salt, making it sweet to the taste, but very good for a thousand other food-type products and even gasoline. Did you know your Toyota may get up and putt from Illinois corn?

Illinois was my only home, and it was all I knew. I grew up in what would be considered a typical Midwestern American home; very ordinary. My parents arrived in "The Land of Lincoln" from Virginia and settled down shortly after they married. It is where they would raise their two children, both of us born in the 1960s. Our various houses were modest and crammed within neighborhoods full of the same type of homes. Dad had his garage stuffed full of a variety of tools for both mechanics and woodworking. The man was skilled in both. Ma was a reader. She also loved fine jewelry. We always had a dog and a cat. I have fond memories of baseball, bicycles, and ice cream trucks stopping in the hood every steamy summer afternoon. Carefree, good times!

Other than the neighborhood bratty girls and boys, my small world of comrades broadened greatly when it came time for school. We had just moved to the Northeast part of the town, which would place me in a different school district. There were new kids from all over the city at school that I would have otherwise never come to know. I would now have to ride one of those big ugly yellow buses stuffed full of loud adolescents heading to a school all the way to the edge of the city limits. One of my first experiences on the bus was of some new kids giving me an attitude over my "southern twang." In my early development at home, I learned my speech patterns in the dialect that Mom and Dad had brought with them from Virginia. I hadn't realized that this wasn't normal for the Midwest. In time, while my parent's accents remained, my hillbilly twang naturally faded.

It was in the first grade when I had my first "girlfriend." Nora and I were in the same class and sat across the aisle from each other. She liked that I was well advanced in drawing for my age. I liked her because she liked my drawings. We spent our "dates" on the playground to see who could burp the loudest. We thought all couples should burp together. Another activity we enjoyed was making rude noises with our armpits. It was a beautiful love story! Nora could run as fast as boys, and I remember thinking that was pretty cool. Maybe she could even run faster than me? I liked her either way.

In reality, Nora was nothing more than a first-grade playmate who happened to be a girl. There was nothing remotely romantic about us, as we couldn't grasp what that even meant. We called ourselves a couple; we defined ourselves as boyfriend and girlfriend because we observed older kids doing the same. We were just mimicking what we saw without a second thought. It was the typical American way, and we thought nothing of it. Looking back now, I can easily conclude that this was a sweet and innocent period where I learned to relate to the opposite sex at a very young age. Nora and I were being "educated" by a self-reliant culture to take romantic desires and match ourselves any way we wanted. Nora and I followed those who went before us without a second thought. This behavior would eventually set me up for a not-so-rosy future in the world of the romantic.

After the first grade, my family moved once again. That meant another school district, so I would never again see Nora. We never "broke up" or said our last goodbyes. Our playground romance faded as if it never was. Life was to go on. But there is one life lesson I took from a little girl named Nora that is worth sharing: Girls have some mad burping skills, and a lot of them are even better than boys. Dare I say they are even louder!

In middle school, the seventh grade precisely, I began to take an interest in girls for real. But I had crawled into a shell of intimidation as females went from playmates to love interests. I was geeky, afraid, and overwhelmed with it all. Junior high couples formed around me, and I observed with great interest. They held hands through the halls, exchanged love letters, and made out in the back of the bus. All this intrigued me, but I was so shy and socially awkward when it came to the opposite sex. Watching this take place made me look forward to the time when I would get to experience young love for myself. There was an occasional crush on my part, but it was always hidden due to my shy nature.

When seventh grade started, I was bussed to a small town some eight miles North of our city. It would be there that my class doubled in size with lots of people I'd never met. What did that mean? New girls! Among those new girls were what I liked to call the "big three": Amanda, Krissy, and Nicole. These girls were ultra-popular, "hottie snotties," highly desired, and they knew it, always hanging together. These females were out of my department, too high up on the totem pole for a "nobody" like me. I would have been considered privileged if they ever chose to as much as speak to me. The "big three" were reserved for upper-class men, dudes who also didn't know that I existed. Still, I always wondered what going out with one of these "sweet thangs" would be like! So, from middle school through high school, I held a secret crush on each one of the "big three" at various times. They never knew.

The high school was adjacent to the middle school, connected by a long hallway. It was a very old red brick building, square in shape with oversized, dingy, faded yellow framed windows. It was nothing to look at. Its hallways were lined with ancient dark blue lockers, most likely from before the days of Moses. One unique feature about this particular schoolhouse, displayed up and down its hallways, hung large framed composite pictures showcasing all the graduated classes from days gone by. Many of these photographs were decades old. In a mere four years, my own picture would also be hoisted above the rows of lockers and trophy cases, memorialized for all those after me to gaze upon.

During these high school years, I made a significant discovery about myself: the love of music. This discovery would be a pivotal moment that would follow me for the rest of my days. I joined my very first band during my junior year, long before you could find instant guitar lessons online. Today, videos of others who have done all the labor of working out very complex pieces of music lay it out so kids, barely able to hold a super strat, can master it with ease. I, and others like me, had to listen intently to our records, doing our best to decipher such things as Stairway to Heaven for ourselves. All that being said, with many first attempts at creating something listenable, our band was miserably awful. But we had an absolute blast being eleventh-grade rockers! To my bandmates, this was nothing more than a hobby, something we could do to pass the time of day. But when I stood in a circle with three other dudes creating sounds from our very own hands and voices, something in me awakened. From that point on, there would never be a time I would not be making music.

At school dances, I would stand in the corner of the gymnasium, watching the "big three" sway and shake with their boyfriends to the hits of the day. When I first decided to go to these events, I would sometimes daydream about dancing with one of them. How stupendous that would be? My imagination was so vivid that I had even picked out a special song we would call our own. Yep, I was that "freak." We would make romantic memories for a lifetime; what a magical night! So now, actually at a dance, I'm lost in wishing for what would never happen.

Now and again, though, I'd experienced a girl having a crush on me. To my surprise, that night, right next to the basketball court, Liz startled me. She wanted to dance! So, do you think I would be thrilled to finally get a chance to wiggle on the free throw line with an actual female and not just daydream on some elevated adolescent fantasy? In perhaps my most outstanding display of complete social inadequacy, I ran away faster than a cockroach under a floodlight. I could go on as there were many more tales of my awkward teen years with the opposite sex, none of them successful or pretty, but I'll spare us all the suffering by not reliving anymore of them.

I was around 16 after my family became Christians, and we began to attend a new church. A couple of teenage girls at this assembly became the objects of my next crushing phase. My first and strongest crush was on a dark-haired cutie named Michelle. Could it be that Michelle would like me too? I would watch her each week while she sang in the choir, secretly wishing I could stir up the courage to talk to her. But at Glenwood Baptist, it was the same old song and dance with me: awkwardness. I had no confidence to say anything intelligent to any of them, so my admiration remained a secret for a long time. Another girl in the youth department named Vicki finally broke me out of this miserable, backward behavior. She was the one who pursued me. To my surprise, despite my self-proclaimed title of a misfit, this girl actually noticed me. Being one who now professed Jesus, my misguided and twisted thoughts told me that if she took a romantic interest in me, it must be the plan of God for my life. Well, hallelujah, Jesus found me a girlfriend. Ahhh! At last, an actual relationship, a girlfriend, romantic love!

I found great adulation in wearing the label of "boyfriend." It felt like I was finally somebody. I discovered self-esteem and values that never existed before. Now, I could walk the hallways at school with my head held high, and nothing would bring me down. One evening, Vicki gave me a necklace engraved with my initials. Surely Heaven had come to earth. The angels were singing praises! I wanted everyone to see what I now wore around my neck. There was a bit of spit and fire in my conversations with my "nobody" friends who were not in relationships. I secretly hoped they would be jealous now that I had a girl. And could there be a possibility one of "the big three" would hear through the grapevine that I was "taken"? Or, could I be seen as being in the same league as they were? Oh, the thought of that was decadent.

Since Vicki went to another school, we had to settle for long phone calls on school nights. Seeing each other was reserved for the weekends and at church. Speaking of church, for us teenagers at Glenwood Baptist, our romances had virtually nothing to do with Jesus. For those of us "in love," the church was just another dating experience. We were there to talk, flirt, and exchange silly love letters. Every week, I would get a nine-page letter written throughout the week of what Vicki was thinking and feeling. While she wrote, she would also listen to the radio and, at the top of her letters, list all the songs that played. I collected quite a stack of love letters from her.

It was in one of those letters that she first proclaimed, "I love you!" When I first read those three words, it felt like they injected me with a euphoric drug. I had finally arrived. I was now someone with actual worth! We had even begun to talk about getting married after school. I found it difficult to imagine life getting any better than this.

I had somehow convinced myself that God had done this for me. Why? We did call ourselves Christians. Because of this, wasn't God obligated to get me a girlfriend so I could be happy? To me, happiness was just that, a girl just for me. Wasn't it God's job to ensure everything works out how I like it? Wasn't He pleased that I had gotten a girlfriend from church instead of school? That was the expectation I had assumed. Life would now be this good forever and ever! Jesus wasn't much more than a vending machine for my enjoyment.

Something was developing in me during this season that wasn't healthy; I was finding my identity in the fact that I was in a relationship. Society told me that being in love was the highest experience I could taste in all of life. Romantic love must be what I desperately needed to measure up to those around me. The bigger picture would say this "relationship thing" became way too important for someone still so very young. Vicki had become the only one who gave my existence substance and meaning. And now that I'd tasted "love," the thought of not having a girlfriend wrecked me. Looking back now, I was addicted not to real love or Vicki herself; instead, I couldn't get enough of how she made me feel. All dudes want to feel desirable and that a real, breathing girl wants to be with them. These emotions would happen between us, and that is what I craved. This "love" was sort of an escape from the not-too-exciting existence of a boring 17-year-old. I had fallen into a definition of love coming from my peers, the silver screen, and culture in general as it constantly preached at us to chase whatever felt good.

Teenage couples were everywhere at Glenwood Baptist Assembly. My thoughts were that those of us in relationships at church were in a holy place because we dated other Christians. But inevitably, both the young couples at school and at church all fell off Cinderella's pumpkin wagon. Breakups. They were bloody and brutal. They seemed to come in droves. Unlike most other splits, Vicki and I never sat down and officially ended things; she just vanished out of my world without hardly a word. She stopped calling and ceased attending church. What had happened? Her treatment confused me. Now, my weekends, usually reserved for dates, were empty. How could a girl who loved me so much now not love me at all? And there it was: a broken heart, my first. Oh, how it hurt!

I only saw Vicki one more time, ever. There was no communication, no explanation. She just returned a gift I gave her one evening and never said a word. I grasped for answers. Now church sucked. School sucked. The 17-year-old life sucked. Out of desperation, I called out to God for the first time in a legitimate way. In my newfound misery, I started to take Him seriously.

I went through some religious rituals when I was younger, assuming I was a believer. Now, with greater clarity, I understood at the time that I wasn't. It was through this stabbing heartbreak that I came to know Jesus for real this time. The Bible says that we all have fallen and cannot save ourselves. God took matters into His own hands and paid the debt of sin Himself through the death of His son, Jesus. When we believe that He did this for us in a personal way, God substitutes His righteousness for our mess and saves us! Jesus rose from the grave to give us new life when we believed. Enough of this religious posturing; I believed for real this time. I understood the cross and believed. I had been doing what I wanted to do, living on my own terms, and it broke my heart.

So what really happened between Vicki and me? Over time, as the clouds lifted, it became clear she was bored with me. Looking back, I would have been bored with myself, too. Fluff love built on nothing but emotional teenage vehemence runs out of steam. It was all that American selfishness about how someone makes you feel. It is the same type of rubbish we are fed daily by the world we live in. It had nothing to do with the true love that cherishes and even suffers for another. No, God had nothing to do with our teenage romance. We did it all on our own. I had to come to terms with the fact that Jesus didn't find me a girlfriend; I did. I had a lot to learn about love.

As the months passed, the bleeding eventually ceased. However, as you'll soon see, that wasn't enough blood for me. Truth be told, I couldn't wait to get out there and find another lady. Maybe this time, God would like the next one I picked!

- K -

Blue Jeans and a Beach Across the State Line

I know you / I walked with you once upon a dream / I know you / That gleam in your eyes is so familiar a gleam / And I know it's true, the visions are seldom all they seem / But if I know you / I know what you'll do / You'll love me at once the way you did once upon a dream

—Once Upon a Dream

Song by George Bruns, Jack Lawrence, and Sammy Fain

That was the song of my heart at seven or eight years old. You could catch me dancing with the robe hanging off the back of my bedroom door while singing "Once Upon a Dream" to my own little romanticizing heart. I had my own kid-size vinyl record player in my room. Shutting my door meant it was just me, my record player, and my long-playing record album of *Sleeping Beauty* with narration and picture storybook encouraging me to imagine being loved by a prince. Over and over, I'd play that story and sing those songs as if I were her, Briar Rose, the sole object of Prince Phillip's affection. A man who would go to great lengths against all kinds of maleficent evils to save me and love me all for himself. I built my hope in romantic love on nothing less than Disney's lie and fatefulness.

I needed something to believe in. It was my first witness of love and dreams coming true. I needed to believe it. I had been trained early in life to believe my childish, plump frame would make me undesirable to men. Loving the likes of me would be too challenging for a guy. Yet, on the other side of the fence, I was also trained to believe that it's what is on the inside that counts. Well, which is it? Inside? Outside? No-sides? All-sides? Ugh! I wanted to be fair and pretty, like a princess. I wanted to be extraordinary, like a queen. Why can't I be both and have one gallant man fight to have me to himself?

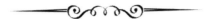

Born and raised in the rolling hills of Iowa, I spent my most formative years in the second-largest city in Iowa. Grant it, Iowa hills are less climbing than Tennessee's, which we now call home. Iowa "hills" have a roll to them. Gary will be rolling his eyes right now at what he thinks is an exaggeration of my imagination. However, I can confidently declare that Iowa is not as flat as Illinois. At which point, he will concur. I don't ever remember Iowa being boring. I grew up in a Catholic family of four. I went to Catholic schools from the first to the eleventh grades. Nuns taught me reading, math, and social studies. Priests taught me religion. I completed all my sacraments unto Confirmation. Waiting for me far into my horizon would be the sacrament of marriage or the holy orders of becoming a nun. The joke around our high school about ex-nuns was that they left their sacred orders because they finally found out what nun (gett'n none) meant. I was definitely holding out for a sacrament of marriage. I was far from either of those opportunities in catholicism when I learned a greater truth.

In Catholic school, I attended services weekly and practiced the rosary, confession, and the stations of the Cross. I also learned etiquette for girls: how to walk, sit, set a table, and wear make-up. Yes! It was in etiquette class that I met Mary Kay, and my fascination with creating illusions of flawless skin began. It's true, Kiss and Alice Cooper have nothing on me. It is also where I had my first romantic experience. I was in the third grade. Boys in school were weird to me. They didn't want to talk. They wanted to play, tease, and poke at you. One boy, in particular, was teasing me a lot. Teddy. One of my girlfriends told me he liked me. What? Why would a boy who likes me tease me? Suddenly, I was awakened to all the little romances happening around me: boys teasing girls and girls giggling over it. Weird.

It felt like a long, hard school day, and the teacher could tell we needed a fun break. She set us up for a game of Heads Up Seven Up. Yes, there is a God! The premise is to call seven kids to the front. The remaining students put their heads down to avoid seeing the select seven approaching. Each of the seven tapped one classmate of their choice on the shoulder. We, in turn, put our thumbs up to signify that we were the chosen ones. Up to that day, I had never been chosen. Too plump, I'd reason and lie to myself. This day was not that day. I felt someone brush by. Deep inside, I was begging for them to pick me. It happened! I felt a quick tap on the shoulder and sensed someone rushing off.

Now, the pressure was on. I would have to figure out who picked me if I wanted to be the following "picker." The teacher called out, "Heads up! Seven up!" The chosen ones stood up to review the cast of seven pickers, and the deductions began. I looked up to see the seven, which included none other than "the Kim-crush'n" Teddy. Could it be? Of course. He had a crush on me. He likes me. He picked me out of all the other third-grade girls. He will be so excited I figured it out, and he'll know I like him too. I mean, I guess I do. If a boy likes you, you gotta like them back, right?

Sister Ann calls my name to make me guess. My heart is pounding out of my chest. If I'm wrong, I will be so embarrassed and have to conclude that Teddy does not love me after all. I dared big time and guessed: Teddy. His cheesy grin dropped. He admitted getting found out and went back to his seat. I was elated. Not only had I had genius insight, but I also had a boyfriend! Oh man, what a day. Someone picked me. I had a boyfriend. And I get to be one of the seven "pickers." It was too much affirmation for my little hopeful heart. The next day, however, I learned Teddy hated me. Why? Because I picked him. It was like I sold him out or something. Ouch! All my new esteem deflated in an instant. That was the day I learned boys don't like smart girls; what's on the inside doesn't count after all.

The rest of my school career was spent in the "fat lane," believing it's what is on the outside that counts. The lie that I was not desirable kept proving its point. No one ever chose me. I spent my school years secretly crushing on a boy here or there, never telling a soul. I never dated. I never went to school dances expecting a date. No homecomings. No proms. It was becoming an excellent setup for the convent life. Marriage or Holy Orders? It looked like the ol' Holy Orders had been written in the stars for this girl after all.

During my junior year, I daydreamed about life after high school. I had some decent artistic talent and considered moving into the graphic arts. I'd be that cool girl with the black t-shirt, DIY bleached torn jeans, and Chuck Taylors, living in a city-size loft apartment with a high ceiling and exposed brick walls. It would be so cool and so far apart from the status quo my dear family found comfort in. That was my dream until I woke up one morning to a new reality: we were moving to Illinois.

My dad had accepted a job transfer with his company. None of us were excited about it. I was one year from graduating into freedom, graphic arts at our community college and fabulous loft apartment living. Not now! I cried for three days. I even considered staying behind and living at my best friend's house from school for my senior year, but something deep inside me would not let me do it. I wonder now if God Himself directed my path to the one state where I would find my one and only husband long before I believed He cared about stuff like that.

Just before I entered high school, my mom had been changing. The best way I could explain it was that she was happier. She was lighter and joyful, just more hopeful. Our Catholic practices had waned down to holiday attendances, and she was spending more time with friends outside our church and going to Bible studies with them. I can remember a time in my Catholic adolescence, kneeling to pray my penance (a token of suffering for my grade school sins) and questioning why. Why did I have to tell the priest my sins? Why couldn't I just tell God myself? Will I ever get to Heaven? Living life without the assurance of Heaven was a heavy burden. There came a very significant day following that contemplation. My mom came into my bedroom on Saturday and shared with me her new hopefulness. She had come to learn a greater truth: You can know that you know you are going to Heaven. What?

.

It had been our experience that a person can never know if they will be good enough to go to Heaven and live in a Holy God's presence forever. We had to live only hoping we would have been good enough in this life to be acceptable to God when we die. The line between what was good and good enough was never very clear. She explained to me that what Jesus did on the cross was more than enough to make us good enough to live with God now and forever when we believed it was enough. I didn't have to live with the fear of possibly going to Hell someday because of a sin I forgot to confess. I'm in! I'm in, not because of anything I could do for God but because of what Jesus already did for me and God. He made me acceptable. There really was a Prince who was choosing me after all. One who desired me to be His own!

I prayed "the prayer" she offered because I wanted to be acceptable and did not want to go to hell. For the first time, I confessed my sins straight to God myself! I remember feeling somewhat new. My insides fluttered a little like a butterfly as something changed. It would be another 14 years before I would have a deeper understanding of what that was all about.

By the time I'm a junior, I'm talking to God a little more. Well, mostly complaining to God, let's be honest. During my complaining petitions to God, I pulled out our encyclopedia. I looked up the city we were moving to. They had a beach. Okay, now that's what I'm talking about—something to look forward to. So, maybe I won't be the artist in a city loft but an artist in a beachfront bungalow; that's cool, too. To sweeten the deal, my parents gave us a choice. We could finish out school at the local Catholic High School or the county public school down the road. All I could think of was jeans. I can wear jeans to school! Public school for my senior year and a beach? Yes, let's do this.

Long story short, four hours after crossing the state line, on our way to our new home, we drove through this itty bitty farmer town with its name painted on its water tower. I could not pronounce it for the life of me. I thanked God I was only passing through; I later learned this was actually the town where I would receive my last year of high school education. To top it off, I went to that so-called "saving grace" beach I had anticipated. Um, two words: tiny and stanky. Stanky, as in where fish came to die, literally. I cried for three more days.

With no promising graphic arts education to continue in (the school's art ed department topped out at the 200 level), no beach parties to look forward to, and, of course, no romantic landscape to speak of, I walked into the unimpressive big square, two-story, old red brick schoolhouse with oversized dingy yellow framed windows. Turning the corner toward the offices, I looked down the hallway. The walls were lined with ancient dark blue lockers, most likely from before the days of Moses. One unique feature about this particular schoolhouse, displayed up and down its hallways, hung large framed composite pictures showcasing all the graduated classes from days gone by. Many of these photographs were decades old. I thought to myself, "Great, in a mere few months, my own picture would also be hoisted above the rows of lockers and trophy cases, memorialized as the senior year transplant with bad wavy hair and fat cheeks, hanging over the lockers with the Class of 1984 embedded into the frame for everyone to gaze upon for years to come." Admittedly, I could be caught gazing upon them myself throughout the week. I mean, those '70s shaggy retro hairstyles alone were worth the glances of silent amusement, right?

SCENE THREE:

MEET ME AT CAMELOT MUSIC

- G -
The Death of Addiction

OVER THE YEARS, I HAD imagined what my wedding might look like someday. One thing I did know was that because of the unconventional way the Heavens were leading me through to holy matrimony, my wedding would also be a distinctive experience, set apart from most other weddings. God wants to show off, not in an arrogant manner, but in a revelatory one. Can we really imagine and understand His goodness to us and His desire for us to know it? I sensed a great responsibility to make sure that each individual who would darken the doors of my wedding would go away, knowing that Jesus made it all happen! I carried this conviction for a long time.

As I stood on a stage with my bride-to-be, I donned a felt top hat and custom-made jacket sewn in deep violet; the unconventional is precisely what was happening. The fun fact in it all was that Kim was the mastermind behind this fanciful display of our wedding. While I've always had a thing for the artsy and theatrical, this time, all I had to do was add my intrinsic touches to her overall vision. We had whimsical trees with oversized violets behind us and a giant pocket watch hung from the ceiling with the time reading 3:34. Kim and I read our vows from an ornate scroll. But perhaps the most impactful element would be a twelve-minute video that shared the story of how God had worked through the history of our lives to bring us to this very day. In fact, it would be the much-shortened version of this same book. The mini-movie made our wedding so memorable; it was the message of what Jesus can do in the lives of those who will believe Him in the arena of the romantic. We hoped that no one would forget this ceremony.

But before hitting the stage, we sat in a private room dressed, ready, and waiting for the crowd to file in. A television monitor was hanging on the wall with a feed from the main auditorium. We watched friends and family being seated. I began to note people I had met at various seasons of my life. Some I had known for a short time, others for decades. Carlton and Sarah sat on the left side. I met them before they were married. They never made this "single" guy feel like a third wheel when I hung with them. Now they would have to deal with an old married guy! Ellie and I shared a love for gothic music, which is mysterious and danceable. She liked to share recently discovered new artists with me. There was Greg and Allie, Rick, Barb, Kayla, and Robert and Sharon, to name a few others. Many of these friends were musicians I'd played with at one time or another. Seeing each of them brought back great memories to me. It was so good to have them all in the same room together.

These were friends who had heard my story, how I had given up self-efforts in finding the romantic and chose to hope in God alone. Some had observed me living this way at various points in my life. Then, there was my longtime buddy, Allen. I watched as he took his seat. Allen had been there for most of it. He was around for my adolescent romance with Vicki and some of the other girls to follow. Allen was one of the buddies who sometimes hung with me on weekends when these relationships would tank. My friend had watched me try and fail and try and fail again. He saw me give the madness up for a life of faith, and tonight, he would see this faith finally pay me back. I was so glad he could make it to my wedding!

Allen and I were the same age. I recalled our much rowdier days when we were young in high school. Honestly, we both despised school. We were not model students. For us, it wasn't the wonderful experience that some recall it to be. Initially, discovering the romantic in those times was a convenient escape before it went sour, but other than that, high school itself was a ball and chain for us both.

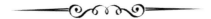

The day was finally here; the ball and chain were about to come off! I slowly strolled the ancient hallways, thrilled that *this* was finally over. Even though I never cared too much for school, it would still be worth one last trip down memory lane. My old locker was over by the gym doorway, clean and bare, awaiting a new tenant next fall. Above my locker was the relic photo of the class of 1955, proudly framed and displayed.

I would miss '55 looking over me each time I dug into my locker. Today was my high school graduation, which I have long since looked forward to. When I finished my final tour, I assumed this would be the last time I would see these hallways. New beginnings! Things felt free in more ways than one. Along with school and the mess with Vicki behind me...could real love be on the horizon?

Many of my peers at school had begun to prepare for higher education. I, for one, had no idea what I was supposed to do with myself, so it was onto full-time employment. But even in the unknown, I could sense there was a destiny for me and that I would find it through God. I had no details of what that may hold yet. It would still be a few weeks until my new job began, so I decided to attend a five-day retreat at a camping facility out in the country. Many friends would be there, some from Glenwood Baptist and others I'd never met. I was hoping for a good time. Secretly, I was curious if I would meet some new girls.

Upon arrival, counselors showed us our beds. They were in rooms that housed about 12, with no privacy. Great, the last thing I wanted was to be stuffed with a bunch of grunting and smelly dudes! While the others unloaded their personals, I lingered around a bit. I had long since gotten over Vicki, but the experience still felt fresh in my mind, I remembered what a disaster it was. I was so grateful that this wreck was over. One thing I knew—I never wanted to go through anything like it again. For the very first time, I paused and asked Jesus to send me the girl He had for me. Somehow, in the simplest ways, I was starting to connect the dots to God and the romantic world. This whisper to Heaven was my inaugural invitation for divine intervention, all at 18 years of age. In retrospect, had I known the magnitude of faith and obedience He would use to answer this simple prayer, I don't know if I would have had the courage to voice such a request.

The retreat proved to be quite pleasurable. There were sports activities, nature fun, and lots of good eats! During volleyball one afternoon, I spotted a pretty "blondie" who always wore an innocent smile. Her name was Cindy. Over the next couple of days, Cindy and I began to get to know each other. I liked her. And just like that, before the week was over, we had plans for our first date. In a repeat performance, as it was with Vicki, my twisted thoughts whispered that if Cindy was interested in me, she must indeed be the plan of God for me. After all, hadn't I *just* prayed for the right girl?

As it turned out, Cindy had to leave the retreat early due to a previous engagement. It would be a couple of weeks until I saw her again. I was looking forward to our date just around the corner. However, I wasn't prepared for what was about to happen next. Michelle, my first crush upon arriving at Glenwood Baptist Assembly a few years earlier, entered the picture again. I was fully fixed on something happening with Cindy when Michelle revealed she had been crushing on me. Whoa! This news threw a wrench in the fan that I never saw coming. Now I had two girls I was into, who both had a thing for me!

Honestly, Michelle would have been my dream and my first choice. We had a small bit of a "relationship" in the short time I was waiting for my date with Cindy. It was brief, innocent, but still romantic. Michelle and I held hands by the campfire at night, sitting close. We had lengthy conversations over frosty bottles of Sprite and Super Slim Jims. Then, we both made sure to join the same sports teams so that we could play next to each other. I would catch Michelle watching me out of the corner of my eye. I wasn't mad about it because I snuck glances at her just the same. But I felt conflicted. I believed I needed to do the right and godly thing and told Michelle that I couldn't continue because Cindy was God's plan for me. She was gracious and sweet. I could hardly believe what I had just done. I said no to this crush I had secretly wanted ever since I first saw her.

For the next year, Cindy and I dated heavily. Things appeared to be going great between us. I worked a job full-time while she finished her last year of high school. And like before with Vicki, I hung my esteem and identity on the fact that I had a girlfriend. Life was a grand old time as long as this relationship went well! In those days, I had no interest in marriage and was content with "part-time" love. That meant I got to hold to the freedom of single life any way I wished when Cindy wasn't around. The other part of the time, I enjoyed "being in love" when I was with her. It was the best of both worlds, entirely on my terms. I still had so much to learn.

Sometime around January the following year, I was in for a jolt. A friend reluctantly told me she had seen Cindy on a date with another guy. He was older and more established than I was. This news confused me, and I didn't know how to handle it. We stopped calling each other, and our dating dried up. There was that familiar hurt that I never wanted to experience again. Daily life became laborious once more when nursing a bleeding heart. A few months passed, and I had begun to get over it. I considered looking for yet another lady and asking Jesus who my next girlfriend should be. And to my surprise, Cindy visited my place of employment on a typical Tuesday afternoon. She wanted me to come to her high school graduation party.

In my clueless mind, I took that as an indicator that God was not through with us yet. Cindy was very affectionate at her party and treated me like we had never stopped seeing each other. The other dude she had been involved with was also there, confusing me. I had spoken to this guy once or twice, and he was a pleasant gent. To be honest, I wouldn't say that I enjoyed face-to-face with my supposed competition, but at the same time, I wasn't even sure where he and Cindy stood. For that matter, I didn't know where I stood with her either. The whole party was this odd mix of questions. Later, Cindy and I had a big talk. She informed me that he didn't mean anything to her and that they were moving on as friends. So once again, we began to date big time. If there was any trace of a broken heart, it was now gone. At the time, you could call me a fool, and looking back on this now, so would I.

The summer came and went rather quickly. Soon, Cindy would be off to her freshman year in college as I continued to work. She spent her next two summers away on mission trips out of the country. Our relationship was becoming more like a long-distance affair. Letters and phone conversations happened often, and we saw each other as much as possible when she was on a break.

Three years have passed since I met Cindy. At one point, I began to notice some strange behavior in her. Cindy just wasn't her fun-loving self. She was now very distant and cold. I didn't know why her entire demeanor and personality had drastically shifted. Of course, it bothered me. While pondering all this one Saturday morning, I had a strong impression wash over me. I knew what was up. Cindy was involved with someone else again, and this time, it wasn't just some innocent dating on the side. How could I have been so undiscerning about this? I confronted her. Cindy confessed the ugly truth to me, even worse than I had imagined. There I was with yet another broken heart. Still very young, I wondered how many more of these I would have to endure. I told myself this was the last time I would have anything to do with her; good riddance, adios. Who knows how many other guys she cheated on me with?

I tried. I swear I did. My logic and common sense said to move on! And how I wanted to. I was getting the idea that God wasn't through with this, and it began to haunt me to the point that I couldn't shake it. So, I sought the counsel of a couple of respected elders in my church. One lady who knew Cindy since she was a little girl informed me of dark things I didn't know about her. As I poured this mess out to another, she told me that God was calling me to pray, to invest myself in intercession over her. I knew that this was what I had to do. I had no idea of the magnitude of spiritual warfare I would face.

Although my ways were not the ways God planned the romantic to work, all I wanted was a faithful girlfriend, a good Christian lady who would love me. Were there any godly women who would stay true? Was that too much to ask? So many guys had their girls; even my pal Allen was now "in love." So why this detour? Couldn't God just sidestep all this madness and get someone to me?

But I couldn't ignore what I knew was before me. I began to hear the Spirit of God whisper to me like He never had previously. He revealed three instructions for me in this season: "Wait, pray, and do not pursue other women." Each day, I entered into long prayers over Cindy. At this time, I assumed that Jesus still wanted us to marry in the future.

This intense ministry of prayer was my introduction to spiritual warfare. It didn't take long for me to get a taste of demonic resistance. It was nasty and gross at times, but it taught me to grow up, stand up, and fight! It was when I discovered that serious prayer is hard work. There would be severe bouts of doubt, that to devote myself to intercede for a crazy girl was maddening. Almost daily, I would feel an intense gloom, negative, nothing but an evil presence. Depression would also haunt me from time to time. The temptation to run from it all was very strong. I'd never heard of anyone else who had a "ministry" as such to a former girlfriend. But I did know that this was from God. I had to persevere. While I did not want to manipulate any of this out of my own efforts, I sensed that it was best not to contact Cindy. There were times when I did see Jesus move significantly on her behalf, which encouraged me to keep at it.

In the bigger view of things, I wasn't sure how much extended intercession was moving in Cindy, but changes were happening in me over time. My feelings for Cindy were being replaced by a single desire to see her free and embrace Jesus. And as a surprise, it didn't matter to me if we ever married now. Cindy called me one afternoon, and we met at a lake the next day. As we sat talking as friends, I had no great attraction to her as I did in the years before; it was revelatory to me. What was happening?

A few months later, I was out with a friend. We sat in my car, listening to music while watching a downpour on a warm spring night. Suddenly, it happened; God lifted my assignment to Cindy! "You're finished." He said it with clarity. There was nothing left in me concerning her. Having all this behind me was exhilarating like a yoke of addiction breaking off me. My future was bright, and I had a new sensation of God being pleased with me. I felt like a new dude, and I was. While I was obeying God, God was changing me. I had given myself to intercession for her for over three years. Now I knew what I had been suspecting for a while: Cindy was not to be my wife. She was never the answer to the prayer for the right girl. That would have to wait.

The break-up with Cindy was not a quick severing. Instead, it was similar to a slow and inevitable death. Anytime you invest yourself in a love relationship, and it dies, it's grievous. It was the second time it had happened between Cindy and me. I'd been down this familiar road before, and the three years of intercession for Cindy had been the catalyst that healed me of any heartache that was left over.

Along with the healing, I now had a full-blown desire for who Jesus had for my future. After finding that my very life was Christ's, how could I begin to consider a lady who wasn't on that same path? I could never return to a selfish pursuit. The greatest thing I gained, my biggest lesson through this time, was when the romance ended with Cindy and God directed me to not search for a new girlfriend. What did this mean? I had been addicted. He had pulled me out of an addiction to the American dating agenda of trying to control my own romantic destiny. God would still keep me in His classroom on the romantic. I knew enough now to get my directives from above and wait for His revelation instead of taking it for myself. And now, for the first time, I had a clue that something was fundamentally wrong with how many Christians were doing romantic love in America.

Oh, the gift of retrospect. The old gymnasium was just as I remembered. It had the same smell. Old buildings tend to smell...well, old. At center court was the large blue Spartan that was a part of my daily life for four years. Today, the symbol was partially covered with folding chairs as friends and family found seats for the class of 1984 graduation. My parents and I squeezed into the bleachers, awaiting the ceremony. This time, it was my sister's turn to don the cap and gown, as it had been my turn five years earlier.

Visiting the old school made me nostalgic. I sat and reflected on those years for a short time when I noticed a few of my peers sitting just below us. They mainly looked the same. Some had a little less hair, others slightly thicker around the middle. We caught up on what had been going on in our personal lives. One of the guys who had been quite a socialite had kept in contact with everyone. He updated me on most of our classmates. Some had moved away. A couple of them had even died within such a short time, which was shocking. Then he informed me about the ones who had married in the past five years. All of this news was a bittersweet experience for me as I knew I'd never see many of these old friends again. Life is like that. Our conversations were cut short once the ceremony kicked off. We had our day as grads, and now it was time for my sister's class to do their thing.

I wasn't the same person who once roamed the hallways at the old schoolhouse. That even included my appearance. Since my interest in music had been growing in intensity, edgy fashion had become important to me. MTV awakened me with a new determination to "represent" my identity as a musician. I recall walking through a local mall and, by chance, spotting a purple pullover shirt with radical green stripes, something a British nu-waver would have strutted. (Think A Flock of Seagulls or Pretty in Pink.) I would own that shirt by the next payday. That awakened me to an entire overhaul of my closet and drawers. Soon, my whole wardrobe would be made over with skinny ties, tweed jackets, lightning bolt shirts, and pins of popular bands covering my jackets. I loved it!

My hairstyle reflected such times with my 1981 mullet with bleached tuffs falling forward down my forehead. It was when that hair statement first arrived and was identified with rockers instead of rednecks and hillbillies. I stood out wherever I went. Later, I found myself drawn to the louder and faster side of musical expression, heavy metal. By now, the clothing had gotten darker and the hair much longer. The Sunset Strip scene had impacted middle America, and I was first in line!

Most purchases of spins were now in the metal genre. I had friends who worked at the Camelot Music store in the mall, and they would play the latest Dio or Maiden just for my ears while I got lost searching the CD bins for some lost treasure of metal heaven.

During the festivities, I looked around at the relic gym with great memories. My thoughts returned to how Jesus had first become real to me during my last year in this very building. Here, He laid the foundational steps for what He would spend the upcoming decades teaching me. The God of the Universe revealed Himself to me through the arena of the romantic, and it was during my concluding year in this place that it all began.

Many of my old classmates were simply five years older, and it was clear to them that I had taken on a new identity in more ways than one. While many of life's questions had yet to be answered, Jesus was up to something in me. My life's trajectory has been altered drastically since being a student here. It brought me excitement! Many of my classmates, by this time, now had husbands or wives. I couldn't help but question: When will it be my turn for love? Could it be that I was a bit anxious? Maybe slightly jealous? As the class of '84 marched across the stage to receive their diplomas, one by one, I was wondering where my girl might be.

- K -
Long Hairs at Camelot Music

Waiting to march across the stage to receive my ticket into adulthood, my 1984 high school diploma, I sat looking over a sea of strangers looking back at me. I was not fully prepared for the life-altering change waiting for me on the other side of the stage. I was just looking forward to summer and finally getting out of school. I had only attended this school for one year. It was hard to get in tight with the people who had grown up with each other since kindergarten. It was like being the new girl all year long. I was not feeling super sentimental until our big varsity linebacker, sitting behind me, gave me a wet willy right in the middle of the ceremony, and suddenly I was flooded with emotion. Okay, I cried like a baby. You know, getting targeted with a wet-willy is equivalent to someone saying, "I love ya, man." I was really going to miss these small-school characters who took to me like a favorite sister of theirs. I learned that small-town friends have the warmest hearts.

Marrying a rock star was my young adult life's dream. I literally stated it in my yearbook memoir. My hopes for the future included being Rick Springfield's secretary. Which, of course, could only lead to marrying Rick Springfield, right? I didn't see Rick Springfield sitting amongst the onlookers waiting to marry me that night, so pursuing an art degree at a small state university would be my plan B until Rick and I got to meet.

I had managed to make it through high school into my senior year, never having a date, let alone a boyfriend. I had a very light list of secret crushes. I tended to dig all-state wrestlers, football linebacker types, and the mysterious, silent, dark "bad-boy" desperado types. None of which ever showed an interest in me. Always a buddy, never a girlfriend, was I. Deep inside, I wanted to be a Pat Benatar type: fierce, sharp, talented, and sexy. Overweight most of my life, crowned with a very wavy strawberry-blond head of hair, speckled freckled cheeks, and having no musical talent did not make for the most rad rocker chick on the block.

That summer ended, and like every other high school graduate, I moved onto a state college campus. I was doing what everybody else was doing, but I didn't understand what I was stepping into when it came to life on my own. Mentally, I was prepared to continue my fine arts education but not emotionally prepared to live on my own. I was terrified. All the incoming freshmen were excited to get away from their parents and party like it was 1999. Literally, that was the song that would thump on the walls of my door room until 4 AM nightly. Suddenly, I was thrust from total parental care to "sink or swim, baby." I had no experience with the life skills required to make college work for me. Overhearing a comment my roommate made when I was pretending to sleep it was clear she had no interest in the fat, shy chick she got stuck with. I would cover my head at night to avoid being caught awake when she came in with her friends in the middle of the night. I feared they would find a reason not to like me, too. I lasted about four days. I hadn't even started any of the academics before I called my dad to come get me.

Everybody has moments in life that break their spirit. That was one of mine. I don't regret leaving. I regret ever going in the first place. I had no real idea that the rest of my life was in my own hands and that I was now fully responsible for making it happen. I went back home as lost as lost can be. All my friends were in college. I had no ambition for a career or a dream of a future. I had no idea why I existed and had no one to help me figure it out. A deep sadness set in, and with it, a new question that would relentlessly knock at my heart for decades to come: What's the point? What is the point of my life? It was a big question that would take another ten years to learn the answer to. All I knew at that point was that I needed to get a job because that's what new adults do. It's what my parents did. I entered the mindless, aimless pursuit of an income.

I landed a sales job at a large retail store called Carson Pirie Scott in the mall. I covered all departments as needed and when needed. My best friend, Michelle, worked there with me her first summer back from college and asked me to go with her to see a new band coming up on the music scene. The show was at a venue called Nashville North on the edges of a small town in central Illinois. We had tickets in the 33rd row. I was excited. I had only been to a handful of small arena rock shows before, so 33 rows back was a pretty decent ticket. Until we got there, that is. Upon entering the venue, I anticipated sneaking up to the middle rows to discover there were only a total of 34 rows. Yep, second to last row we were. It didn't matter because it was the best rock show I had been to yet. The zebra-striped spandex! The black leather fringe! The BIG long hair! I was in love, and being a fan girl from the back row would not be good enough for me and we made our way to the front of the stage. I was enamored and I had to meet this band.

After the show, Michelle and I ran outside to see if we could find the band's bus. Instead, we found a plain yet suspicious van. We hung out for a bit, thinking someone almost famous would surely show up. No one showed but a driver. Frustrated, I started to walk around to the side of the building. I turned back to see where the van might be heading. Just as I passed by an unmarked side door, I heard someone trying to push it open. I stopped to avoid getting knocked out by it and saw him, the frosted mane lead singer! Too dreamy to be true, he looked back at me with this bright, big, beautiful Italian smile and said, "Hi!" Stunned by the perfect timing, the hidden one-on-one chance to see him face to face, I smiled back and said, "Hi," just as that van pulled up. That ended up being the first of three perfectly timed opportunities to exchange "hellos" with none other than rock-throb Jon Bon Jovi.

Growing up, I was always infatuated with musical entertainment. Keith Partridge was my first childhood musician crush. I still practice singing along with, right into my hairbrush of course. I always had this innate desire to know these artists, not just to like them as a fan or follow their music; I wanted to know them personally. I wanted to hang with them, understand what made them tick, and be their confidant. My brush with a rockstar celebrity that night at Nashville North was my first taste of how possible this could be. That was the highlight of my summer and almost a prophetic shadow of things yet to come for me.

Back at the mall, I had my eye on the cosmetic department, but it was more of a prestigious position in retail because commissions and some skill in the art of beauty were involved. I had some talent for make-up, and after a while, my secret desire came true. I assisted the counter manager at the top selling line of make-up. Our counter was front and center to the entire mall! It was the 1980s, and the mall was where all the young adult action was.

Being front and center of the mall, my store got a lot of foot traffic, and the traffic that interested me the most was the boys. I was never one who was given to flirtation. Given more to destiny, I always had a deep assurance that the right guy would recognize something in me worth pursuing. The "prince looking for his princess," right? One night, it happened. Well, I was hoping it was happening. Two guys came up to the counter, being playful and cute. They asked if I'd be cruising the main city street after I got off. I was. I had a delightful 1976 bright yellow Volkswagen Bug convertible that I and two other girlfriends would cruise in on the weekends.

We met up a few times, and we'd all hang out at the Dairy Queen. Eventually, we'd move on to parties or find an abandoned country road to hang out, listen to music, and sip some beers. I grew a maddening crush on one of those boys. Will. His sarcasm was infectious. He was super cute and intriguingly thoughtful at times. He was one of those crushes that consumed your every thought.

We had so much fun hanging out; our sense of humor fit perfectly. We'd talk over the phone during the week about nothing or about what we were watching on TV that night. Soon, his interests became more evident, and they were not in me. He wanted my best friend, Michelle. She was loyal and had no intention of returning any interest his way because she knew I liked him a lot. Once she left for college, I learned her loyalty fell short. She had made secret trips to see him and couldn't help but have sex with him, too. My broken spirit broke again. I was not so much hurt by him not liking me back; sadly, my self-hate was in full bloom, and I couldn't blame him. I was deeply devastated by Michelle's betrayal and her secrets. I never cried over a broken friendship as hard as I cried over that one.

My experience in love throughout my young adult life remained nothing more than that of a wallflower, always crushing, always hoping, never experiencing any of it.

After a couple of years at the make-up counter, I got an offer from the other end of the mall, a store called Camelot Music. It was a record store where I would be a part of the music industry and its history when vinyl records bowed down to cassette sales, eventually giving way to the phenomena called CDs. The music industry had called my name, and it felt so right. I was in! I was moving closer and closer to that high school Rick Springfield destined marriage.

I loved working at the music store. The "long hairs" and the "no-collars" always came in. "No Collars" were the dudes who took low-end part-time jobs, mostly in food service, because they were in bands that planned to be rock stars someday. I met lots of music lovers like myself, and my social life was starting to take a new breath of life. One "long hair", in particular, launched me into a whole new era of musical taste. This guy would come in like all the others to see what was new. His hair would hang down over his face as he filed through the heavy metal CD bins. He was an unassuming type of presence. He was the only "long hair" who would not peek back through his hair to see who was checking him out as the others did. That was key! I knew this guy was authentically cool; he was in it for the music, not the attention. I just had to know him, so I pulled up all my girl power and introduced myself. He was as cool as I had assessed, and he invited me to check out his band that night...*and* meet his cute wife. Ugh!

So the cool rocker dude was married, but that didn't stop me from taking him up on his invitation to check out his band. I pulled on one of my many rocking black t-shirts, slipped into my DIY bleached torn jeans and Keds (I needed gas money more than Chuck Taylors), called up a couple of my girlfriends, and off we went. I was smitten. This band was hard, intense, and serious about their groove. The best part about meeting them was that I became more than a fan; I became a friend, and they became my family. They were the most popular band in town and ran the roads throughout the region. I ran with them. I found my tribe! When I wasn't there, they felt it. I knew them personally, hung with them and understood what made them tick. I was a confidant of theirs. It was like I found something I was made to do. I was made to be a Band-Aid. You'll get the reference if you've ever seen the movie *Almost Famous*. If you haven't, stream it, and then you'll get the reference.

These years felt full to me at my most carnal of existence. Sure, it involved alcohol, a little recreational smoking of funny cigarettes, lots of late nights, and not being sure how I got home. When living according to the flesh, sin is always fun for a season; the Bible tells us so. However, one thing remained unmoving in me: I desired an enchanting love story, a destined kind of love. I dug my new tribe, but there was a lot of "sex without love" going on all around me. I stood out because I simply could not escape my initial desire: to wait for love. I don't know what it was. All my girlfriends had no problem sleeping with the next opportunity that came their way. I couldn't. The pressure was always on. My girlfriends would tell me, "It's no big deal. It's just physical." However, those conversations would eventually reveal their regrets. They'd end up confessing they couldn't stop it. They'd wished they could, but after the first time, it was like a drug addiction, and they couldn't say no to it anymore. The more I saw their shallow relationships, heartbreaks, and drama, the more determined I was to wait for love.

SCENE FOUR:

AT THE CROSSROADS

- G -
Hypnotic!

O H, THAT SOUND! HYPNOTIC! MESMERIZING! Addictive! There was simply nothing like that sound, and I've never gotten over it, even to this day. However, music was not my first passion. As a young lad, my obsession, like so many young boys, was athletics; for me, it was mostly baseball. I couldn't wait to slide into my little league uniform during sizzling July days. With its pinstripes and number proudly displayed on the back, that uniform made me feel like I was a big deal. The hours spent dreaming of long dingers at Wrigley are too many to recall. I just loved baseball. But around age 14, another love was about to be realized. My parents recently gave me a radio all my own. WLS Chicago, with all the current hits, never stopped in my little bedroom. It was what all the teens listened to. My young teenage life now had a soundtrack. My early fave was Elton John, who had elaborate costumes and outrageous eyewear. My first musical purchase was a used Elton 8 track for $1.79, bought with my own cash. Now, I didn't have to wait for the radio; I could do the "Crocodile Rock" anytime I was in the mood!

It was only a short time before I was replacing E.J. as my preferred spin. Down in the basement bedroom of my older cousin hung a dozen photos of four dudes in sinister-looking clown-like makeup and long dark hair. Never had I laid eyes on such a dangerous, flamboyant, and compelling band. I'm sure you know whom I'm referring to...Kiss. With my adolescent eyes fixed on the glossies, I found them both disturbing and alluring. These were the days before Kiss was an American icon. The days when they were considered nothing short of dangerous. Most parents wanted to steer their kids far away from this Kabuki carnival. Later, a buddy my age had his parents' permission to crank their console stereo, and he spun the Kiss *Alive* album for me. That Saturday afternoon was when I first heard the sound that would inspire me even to this day: the distorted electric guitar! It began that day with Ace and his smoking Les Paul, but it would hardly end there. Soon, I would be into Zeppelin, Sabbath, Aerosmith, and all the heavy rock staples of the mid to late 70s. I would eventually graduate to the Los Angeles Sunset Strip to Van Halen, Ozzy with Rhoads, Ratt, and many other "big hair" slingers of the 80s. Thrash pioneers Metallica, Megadeth, and Iron Maiden eventually found their way to my listening palette, and Prog pioneers Rush, Queensryche, and Dream Theater. I was fixated on heavy guitars!

As much as the heavier side of song was my most significant musical crush, many Nu-wave and alternative artists of the era would also grab me. The Cure, Dead or Alive, Flock of Seagulls, and countless others were frequent spins. Pop music of the day was also a thing for me. I was pretty diverse in my taste.

I found an expression I could identify deeply with within the art of music. In the early days, it was only a fantasy to think that I could actually be someone who makes music. One of my good friends shocked me the summer before my senior year when he brought home his own cheap knockoff of a Les Paul. I found it hard to fathom that he actually took the initiative to attempt to become a real musician and not just dream about it. My buddy made me jealous, and I wouldn't let him have all the fun with a real guitar. The next day, I emptied my bank account and brought home a Japanese version of a Fender bass! Spending countless hours, I began to develop my ear by playing along with many of my records. My poor parents lost their minds as the walls shook from my bedroom from the extra low-end rumbling.

Then it happened. It was a day that changed everything. A friend from school heard that I was now a budding four-stringer. He and a pair of other dudes were forming a band, and a Fender bass was exactly what the band needed. The evening that the four of us stood in a semi-circle and struck those first chords was revelatory for me. The "music" we created that night was horrible, as you can imagine, but it was beautiful to me. I couldn't stop thinking, "Listen to us. We are doing it. We are making music." I, Gary, was a legitimate musician! The joy this gave me was nothing I had ever experienced before. That night, I found a significant element of my purpose!

Our little high school garage band went nowhere and ended when our high school graduation came. However, that didn't stop me; from then on, I would always be involved in some musical endeavor, playing all the time. I also transitioned from the bass to the electric guitar as my main instrument.

As mentioned, during my senior year in high school, I legitimately came to faith in Jesus. A legit faith in the work of Christ on the cross and His resurrection was a revelation to me. I believed! After some time, I began to sense a more significant reason for music in my life other than what was typical. At this time, I discovered Jesus rock, bands, and artists that used louder, more aggressive forms of songs to express Christian beliefs and convictions. I dove right into this new discovery.

Somewhere are a few photographs of a friend and myself as we lit fire to our "secular rock." We were giving up this worldly music that would tempt us to be involved in things not so good for us. It was a big trend for those times. We decided to consume only Christian rock and pop. Looking back, this was most likely a good thing for me for where I was at the time, but now I see it as somewhat extreme, and I'm not too sure I would repeat such an act if I had it to do all over again. I threw away hundreds and hundreds of dollars worth of music. It's worth mentioning that I eventually re-purchased everything I initially struck a match to. Nevertheless, as for me, the songs that I would now write and play would hold some eternal message pointing to Jesus in one way or another. Although I don't much care for the term "Christian band," all the groups I would become involved with would be ones that communicated such a more profound message than the covers of the Crue, Led Zep, or Guns and Roses.

It's somehow the nature of the music world that people idolize musicians. The guy who drives the ice cream truck won't get a second look from desired women, but let him strap on six strings, and something changes. Put him behind a microphone, and it's a different tale. It is certainly true for mainstream acts, and in many instances, this scenario is no different for the musician just because he believes in Christ.

One of the early Jesus bands I was in played often at a local club. The room would be full every time we plugged in, many of these being girls. When I adorned my zebra-striped pants and slung my black tricked-out Strat over my shoulder, much more female attention came my way than when I walked through a department store in Levi's. Girls liked boys who rocked, even if they loved Jesus.

While I hoped our band could have a significant impact, it stalled, so I moved away, hoping to find another gig in greener pastures. Eventually, I played a few gigs with a very eclectic group of people, but it was nothing serious. And later, I auditioned for an up-and-coming Jesus metal band. Nothing was very compelling about them, and I never heard from them again. It was then that I heard God whisper concerning music, "I want you to just wait for me. Don't try to make any of this happen for yourself." So I ceased looking for a band and played guitar in my bedroom, learning Stryper songs.

One evening, I received an unexpected call with an invitation to play in the band that I had initially left. Since then, the band had reformed with another guitarist, and he had just made his exit. The band had begun to gain some attention in the current Jesus metal world. If I rejoined, the stages for this band would be bigger than they had been, and I knew this would surely get me greater female attention. My logic told me this was sure to introduce me to my wife. I had this all mapped out in my head. While I enjoyed signing autographs and taking pictures with the pretty girls, my core desire was to find "the one." During our run in those days, some women didn't hear our message as much as they liked our wild clothes and long hair. They treated us like any other band: very forward. I could see through this most times and steer clear of such traps.

We did some regional traveling, mainly opening for more prominent bands on tour. The entire experience was full of great times but never did produce Mrs. Right. It took me some time to discern what had happened here. There were two distinctive dynamics. First, I was now on a divine agenda in the realm of love. The work of the Spirit in me would not allow me to compromise for one of the forward girls who paid attention to me simply because I was a six-stringer under stage lights.

God had canceled that whole romantic circus, and the ship had sailed. Second, even though I functioned on a high-profile stage where girls liked boys who rocked, I experienced being hidden from the true gift from Heaven because it wasn't yet the season for such a gift, and no amount of hairspray would change that!

- K -
God, Help!

Being a "Band-Aid" meant you were with the band for the sake of music, not the guys. There was, however, one guy in the band who stood out to me over the others. I don't think it was just the rocking long hair; all the guys had that. I don't think it's because he was a guitar player; after all, they had more than one. No, it was more of his kind nature and his fun-loving sensibility. When everyone was acting all crazy, he had the best, fun-loving ways to bring everybody back to their senses, even if just for a moment. He had a level head on him, loved tacos, and never met a stranger. He was the one guy in the band I got to have thought-provoking conversations with. We became good friends, and eventually, he became more than a friend; he became my pastor.

A week after Gary and I announced our engagement, my pastor, friend, and ex-band brother, Jeff, called me. He wanted to hear all the details of how Gary came to know I was to be his wife. He was managing some astonishment as his many responses within our conversation were catching up with pauses in search of words. Understandably, we went way back and saw each other through a lot. I saw him come to Christ, grow into a beloved worship leader, become a father twice, and eventually become a pastor who planted a church. I partnered with him and his wife in what became one of the fastest-growing churches within our denomination east of the Mississippi River at that time. They both carried with me my hope to marry someday and loved on my vibrant, pre-teen daughter, Andee, as though she was their own.

Oh, did I mention my daughter yet?

So, how does a girl determined to wait for love become a single mom? Well, it's called a long story and now a book called Choosing Life After Rape. Running with the band, I sometimes found myself in compromising situations. When things got too close for comfort, I'd pray within myself for a way out. "God, help!" was as poetic as my prayers would get. God was my life-saver at best. Anne, my best friend then, would roll her eyes at me and accuse me of being ridiculous in asking God to do me a favor since I was also one who got myself into trouble. It's all I knew of Him at that time. I knew Him as a God who saved me from my troubles. I had yet to know Him as a God who keeps me out of trouble.

I remember one night in particular. Anne and I went to a street celebration downtown with a group of girls. This massive city-wide event closed out our sticky, humid summers every year. Tens of thousands would come in for the food, the bands, the crafts, the wares, and the rides. We girls had a bad habit of drinking wine coolers at someone's house before we went out. It put us in the party mood while saving us money at the bars. This night was no different. We drank, went out, had a good time, and eventually learned of a nearby party. We made our way through the masses of hot and bothered people back to our car. Somebody had brought some pot for that night, and we were all happy to indulge before leaving the parking lot.

Parking was tight and awkward. It was difficult to maneuver through crooked, parked cars and people walking all around, especially when you're buzzed. We finally got our opportunity to pull out onto the street and into the line of cars waiting at the stop sign. It appeared that getting out anytime soon was going to be impossible. The vehicles slowly inch forward, waiting their turn for the upcoming intersection. We were all busy laughing, talking about cute guys, and growing impatient when we suddenly heard a loud thud. Anne, who was driving our car, started to freak out. She accidentally rolled into the car in front of us. Panic hit all of us like a freight train. Our brains were trying to catch up with what just happened and what to do about it. Paranoia took the lead, and I started to imagine cops coming, being a headline on the local news, going to jail, and shaming my parents to no end. My head returned to the thought of cops. "Oh no," I thought, "we've still got pot in the car!"

Immediately, of course, when you're high, nothing is immediate. I figured I'd stuff the bag of pot into the backside of the brake light compartment in the rear window. Anne exits the car, hoping to appeal to the woman we just hit. When she returned, she told us we were the third car to hit her today. The woman had let everybody else off the hook, but no more. She was calling the cops this time! Anne said she thought she knew her from the retail store Anne managed, so she would try to appeal to her one more time. I get my "inside" prayers going; you know which one. The only prayer I knew: "God, help!" I was praying it over and over again like rapid-fire bullets spraying the Heavens. Anne finally returns to the car and says, "I don't know what just happened, but she changed her mind and decided to let us go." What? No way! NO WAY!

Partly drunk, a little stoned, and mostly stunned, I could not believe what had just taken place. Anne returned to the driver's seat, and everybody was excited to hit the party. Not me; I was stuck in a severe state of disbelief. I suddenly became overwhelmed with a new truth: we were so undeserving of that favor, so ridiculously undeserving. My mind could not comprehend it, and I began to weep uncontrollably.

I tried to explain to my friends how I prayed, and God answered. I tried to explain how deeply I was knowing we did not get what we truly deserved because God spared us. They were not getting it, but I was getting wrecked in my heart. That encounter with answered prayer sobered me up in an instant. I sat in the backseat, utterly detached from all the other party chatter, and stared out the back windows, knowing in the most real way that I had just had my first experience with God's mercy. He had never been more real to me than in those moments. The only person who would have appreciated it, but in no way could I tell, would have been my mom. It would have broken her heart to know what I was up to, though I'm sure she had suspicions. She was at home that night, probably praying, too, for God to save me, but in a whole other way than just being saved from the cops.

Looking back on that event, I can see that was not the only time I didn't get what I deserved. With an event this dramatic, it would have been a good time to turn from being followed by God and to start following Him back. Nope, not yet anyway; it did, however, prepare a place for me to return to because what was next would be more life-changing than any night in jail would have provided.

It was a three-day Easter weekend, and Anne and I were looking for something fun to do. Anne was adventurous when it came to certain guys, and our conversations frequently rolled around to how unadventurous I was. It was weird, but on this particular day, I had finally embraced the idea that love could be written into my destiny, and I would not chase it down. At 26 years old, never having had a boyfriend, I should have felt desperate by now. Still not seeing true love resulting from all the sex happening around me, I became more willing to wait for destiny to set me up, and I said so.

Anne was not buying it, even perceived some self-loathing in my so-called excuses, and said so. Admittedly, there was some of that self-loathing going on. Maybe my hope did come from the idea of it being impossible for someone to desire me. Whether she was right or wrong, I didn't care. All I knew was that I wanted to rest in something greater than myself. I drew a line in the sand that day; I was going to stop doubting that love could be destined.

We spent that day strolling some throwback shops. I have always favored retro 50s and 60s vibes. I loved the perceived innocence of guys courting girls; the bashful social etiquettes and fashions seemed glamorous to me, and I had a deep affinity for mid-century modern styles. I should say I have an affinity for MCM and have continued to stage all my living spaces with as many MCM accents and treasures as tastefully possible.

Well, that evening, we planned to dine out and find a place to dance afterward. Anne grew an interest in a bartender, and I had a feeling I'd be on my own at some point before this evening ended. Our waiter that night was friendly. I guess he was too friendly because, according to Anne, he was showing some interest in me. I did not pick up on it, but she quickly brought it to my attention and strongly encouraged me to get over my self-loathing and entertain it. I wasn't attracted to him, but now there was pressure to be, or at the very least, to be attracted to his interest in me. You know, be flattered and flirt with the guy because he started it.

The best I could do was be friendly and invite him to hang out and dance with us after he got off work. The waiter showed up. He had made several advances on me throughout the evening that I politely pushed away. Even though I had predicted it, I still got a little miffed when my friend snuck off with the bartender. So, when the waiter learned I liked live music, he invited me to go with him to see a live band near his place. I had no reservations. I would sometimes see live bands by myself, and I believed I had well proven my disinterest in this guy by this time. I had every expectation that he'd respect that.

The live music ended as we entered the new "party" destination. I was disappointed and getting irked with this guy now. I ordered myself a drink. Within a few minutes, he came up behind me and pushed it away, insisting I drink the one he "bought" instead. Next thing I know, we are walking back to his apartment building to "get me a cab". I, however, was not walking well. My body felt very lethargic, and my mind was cloudy. I remember him making advances again and me pushing him away again, saying no. I did not know what was overcoming me at the time, but I was beginning to feel I was in trouble.

I woke up the following morning with my head pounding as I gazed around an unfamiliar room. Slowly putting the events of the night before together, I started to become afraid I would not be able to get back to my friend. I got myself together as fast as I could. This waiter dude, who acted like it was just another fun night out on the town for him, called a cab. I headed back in a state of shock. When I knocked on the door, Anne was picking up the phone to call the police. She asked me where I had been and what had happened. With my insides quaking and my head pounding, I whispered words I never imagined I would be saying—"I was raped."

As much as that may appear to be the ending of my innocence, it was simultaneously an unexpected beginning. One month later, I learned I was pregnant, and I prayed, "God, help!" This traumatic event was the final event that returned me to that great mercy I encountered months earlier in the backseat of a smoked-filled car of party girls.

Choosing life by God's grace enabled me to give up living my life my way and hand it over 100% to God to do more than save me from trouble this time. I asked Him to save my whole life, and I asked Him to keep it, too. For the first time, my life was no longer my own. My daughter was His, my past was His, and now our future was His.

SCENE FIVE:

THE MATCHMAKER

- G -

Chicago and Southern Preachers!

I HAD BEEN OUT OF HIGH school for a few years; it was time for a major change. Originally from central Illinois, Chicago was now home to me, where I was hoping a music career might take off. I had found where I wanted to be with no plans to leave. Having already lived in two suburbs, I recently moved to a third, and this was where I discovered my groove. It was the perfect balance of private neighborhood and busy urban edge. After leaving the driveway, you could head left and hit the Loop in no time. Turn right, and after a bit of a drive, find yourself in sparse, open land. In my opinion, it was not far from the best of both worlds. Why would someone who enjoyed both urban madness and quiet seclusion ever want to leave?

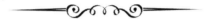

I find something about old-school preachers, especially from the Deep South, compelling. The volume of their voice, the charm of their dialects, and their entertaining personality are just too much to not pay attention to. Maybe it's because I heard my share of this brand of a proclaimer of God's Word when I was younger that makes me think of simpler times. Comfort preachers? I've heard of sillier things. If I run across one on the radio, I'll stop and remember earlier days. Like anyone full of revelation, these older preachers from the American South often have many profound and significant things to say!

I had found a church I preferred in one of the Western suburbs. It was, at most, nine miles from my home. My best friend at the time and I both attended this church. We eventually got involved in church functions and activities such as helping with teens, Bible studies, and swatting balls on the church softball team. Speaking of softball, my buddy and I were quite a kick in the pants for the team, so much so that we brought home the church's first-ever Chicago league championship for churches. That was a great time. Somewhere stuffed away in storage is my old uniform from that team. I pull it out now and again and relive those days!

Both of us also became close with several of the families there. This place was excellent at welcoming singles by having families take them in. They welcomed us as one of their own in this way. These were very good church experiences for all the single peeps.

The Thomas family was one of my faves. Gene and Cathy Thomas were cool urbanites who enjoyed all things "big city." Even though they resided in the suburbs, he was a big deal at the Chicago Art Institute downtown. We dug hanging out with the Thomas family. But to my surprise, despite being a big city boy, can you guess what else Gene dug? Old-time Southern preachers. Can you believe it? What a contrast. I never understood how this urban cool cat would be into the likes of hillbilly gospel. I'm sure glad he was. With what had to be divine providence, Gene introduced me to an obscure preacher from way down in Alabama who would play a significant and pivotal role in my future. Everybody now! "Sweet home Alabama / Where the skies are so blue / Sweet home Alabama / Lord, I'm coming home to you!" (Songwriters: Ronnie Van Zant / Gary Robert Rossington / Edward C. King, Sweet Home Alabama lyrics © Universal Music Corp., Emi Full Keel Music, Emi Longitude Music, Songs Of Universal Inc.)

This preacher guy was both old-time and old-school, very thick with the accent and very compelling at the same time. But some of the things he said set him apart from the rest. This guy drew me in to hear more and more. He offered free transcripts of his various teachings, sermons, and cassette recordings. But it was one series of teachings that caught my interest. A collection of cassette tapes on the biblical principles of the right man for the right woman. What was this? Does "right man" and "right woman" mean what they sounded like? I had to find out. Immediately, I ordered them, eight tapes in all.

When the package arrived two weeks later, I devoured them immediately, multiple times. His "right man and right woman" principles meant exactly what I had hoped they had meant and much more. Never before had I heard anyone teach from the Holy Bible that God Himself had always planned to be directly involved in the romantic arena. It was my first introduction to the truth that the Almighty not only cared about love between humans but actually *wanted* to take the responsibility of matchmaking! What a profound concept this was to my young mind. Chicago, Gene Thomas, and Southern preachers would be the catalysts pointing me not only to my wife but also to our purpose together. All I had to do was follow His lead into the romantic! However, His leads were never anything I could imagine for myself.

Once, visiting central Illinois, my parents met me at the front door with hugs waiting. It had been a few months since my last visit, so we had some catching up to do. They both looked good, enjoying life. An hour or more passed when Ma said she had something for me. She left the room and returned with something I found unusual: a job application. It was to work for a new auto plant recently built in a city less than two hours South of Chicago. It took me by surprise because my mother knew I wouldn't leave the city for something such as this. I was waiting for a coveted new job to open at O'Hare airport that had been promised to me by a good friend's father, who was employed there. So, there was no interest in this car manufacturer.

Nevertheless, to appease Ma, I reluctantly completed the application. She would turn it into the proper people next week. There would undoubtedly be tons upon tons of applicants. I hoped I would get lost in the crowd and my application would be forgotten.

It's funny that when God has plans for you to follow His lead and they go against what you think you want, you may end up eating your words, which is precisely what I did. A little spicy mustard on that, please! Never had I experienced such a turnaround, resulting in so many closed doors. Something was indeed stirring. To make a long story short, everything Chicago had previously provided for me had just dried up all at once. It wasn't just some circumstantial happenings turning in unfavorable ways; I knew God was behind this. My promised gig at O'Hare vanished, and my current job had legal issues. My best friend, whom I spent much time with, was severely injured in an accident, and I was losing my current housing. Decisions had to be made on each of these fronts like yesterday. What should I do?

There was intense pressure to make some moves, but I needed to hear what Jesus wanted for me. I prayed a lot and waited because that was all I could do. I was tempted to worry and wanted to panic—I needed to make a move of some kind very soon. Then I got a call. My old band wanted me to consider returning to central Illinois. That would mean one thing that I didn't want: moving back. But this was the only light, the sole opportunity. I was torn. I was thrilled to strap on my Jackson Super Strat and rock again but was so sad to leave my Chicago world. However, I had no other choice; the voice of God was in that phone call. What I could not see then was that the Almighty had plans I was blind to. He wasn't asking me to plan my own life for Him to bless it. I was responsible for following Him as He led, regardless of where that may be. Could it be that a wife of His doing would not be found out and about in other places, including the Windy City? Could it be, maybe just maybe, she was in the very city I had left in the first place?

Amid this band thing, another unexpected bit of news came my way. Remember how the long-lost idea of this auto plant job was my mother's doing? That company sent me a very thick package of information because they were interested in hiring me. But this was different than just having a quick interview and starting on Monday morning. I had to go through formal testing. The entire process would take nine months. So, move I did. Back in Central IL, while waiting for this job offer, I worked for a Park District in the maintenance department of a golf course. It was seasonal, so the winter months allowed me to do short tours with the band. I lived on our city's Southwest edge with a buddy and was hardly ever home.

The band did its thing for some time, and we went at it hard and fast; we had a blast! We shared Christ in spandex! Lycra missionaries! With all the attention we were getting from touring bands that we played with, I was sure we'd be the next hot commodity in Heaven's metal, and eventually, we would be offered a record deal. We carried that expectation for some time, and the band did create a stir for a while. But then the unexpected happened. Clearly. I heard the whisper of God: "I'm finished with you here." It threw me back for a minute. My run with the band was to be over. I never saw this coming, not at all, with no advanced warning of any kind. My passion, commitment, and work to make this group the best it could be vanished at once. Soon, I would announce this to the rest of the band. I gave them my resignation, and I played my last show. All of this aligned with the auto manufacturer's schedule to complete their assessment of me. The company finally pulled the trigger on me and offered me a job.

I took the offer and I started working at the auto factory. I also began to make some very good money! Who wouldn't want that? It was something that I never would have chosen from my own wisdom. Looking back, I can say that the Almighty was busy directing my path outside of my own understanding. As I saw it then, there was no harm in giving it a shot for a short time anyway. But the only thing was that a short time inevitably turned into a very long time. It was a season of life where so many events were happening suddenly and unexpectedly. Jesus was driving this thing without me asking, and honestly, I wasn't too thrilled with His decisions for me.

- K -
"There Will Be a Man..."

"There will be a man who hears My voice." My mom was pivotal in my family coming to the revelation of all Christ has done for us. Her own experience with that truth led her into a deep and abiding relationship with Christ that made her know Him and know His desires. She was a picture of submission to God's will, what praying without ceasing looked like, and what it looked like to hear from God. She heard from Him in profound ways. Ways that made you want to be near her. She had been praying in her bed one morning when she came to me in the bathroom as I was giving my newborn daughter a sponge bath. She had been asking God to provide me with a husband ever since I brought my baby girl home. This morning, He responded to her prayer: "There will be a man who hears My voice."

I trusted her. I was new to the ways of God, and she was my teacher. I was new to what it meant to hear from God and all a promise from Him can entail. What she brought to me of His words was more than a sweet sentiment of hope and a future. It was an invitation into a divine mystery, a love story penned with sweeping thrills, great suspense, unbelievable overcoming, and winning more than first imagined. A love story ultimately designed to transform me and make me know Him. Better yet, to love Him.

Of course, I didn't know that from the get-go. I heard, "There will be a man..." and ran out to buy a new outfit for church the next Sunday! Seriously, a cute pink-pastel shorts-suit. Soft and sassy and ready to marry. I wore it four Sundays in a row to prove how determined I was to believe those words. I attended a young adult Sunday school class, and by the end of those four weeks, my promised husband had not shown himself, so I figured I better change it up before someone thought me to be really weird. After all, I was only a little weird. By week five, I'm looking around the room, measuring compatibilities. I glance over to the girl sitting next to me, and my eyes drop to her digging in her purse. She was counting her birth control pills. Wait? She's a Christian, right? What is she doing? That was my first glance into the old reality of living in a new environment. Christianity does not immunize you from the temptations to pursue a love for yourself.

Deciding to have my baby and then to keep her was proving to be the right decision each and every day I walked into it. I loved my daughter. She was a pure delight and a vital key God used to heal me from the event that attempted to ruin my heart and my future. On my first Mother's Day, God inspired my mom to buy me a crystal bud vase and some silk violets to display in it. She did not know why. All she knew was that I was to take them to work and keep them on my desk. So I did. As I write this, I can see how sweet God was to teach me to hear and obey by using my mother's example first. He used someone I loved and trusted while I learned to love Him, trust Him, and hear Him for myself.

I had been reading the Bible as a discipline. I did not understand much of what I was reading, but I wanted to ensure I was doing everything right so that I wouldn't disqualify myself from getting what He promised: a husband. A husband was foremost on my mind and in my prayers those days, so when I kept coming across the word "purple" in my readings, it struck me strange that such a common color would be noted in such ancient text. It struck me: purple as in violet as in violets. God was highlighting that color in His Word to bring to my attention those violets pointing to His royalty and authority over my promise. Those violets were to be a reminder that a man will hear His voice because, like a king ruling over a country, promises happen simply because He said so.

Every day I went to work, those violets reminded me that He had not forgotten what He said: There will be a man. Hundreds of wild violets popped up in my parent's backyard that spring, and my hope was renewed. He will do this! My mom believed this, too. My daughter and I continued to live at home with my parents. As my income did not provide enough for us to live on our own, and it worked out for our good in many ways. My daughter got to start her life in a family environment; we were guarded and protected, our needs were supplemented there, and best of all, I was discipled into a relationship with Christ by my mom. Our relationship deepened during that time like never before. Her wonder and excitement over Jesus were infectious. Her profound understanding made me stop in my tracks, constantly reminding me that my life is not about me. Both my parents got to experience daily the joy my daughter was born to bring. Little did we know that the first four years of my daughter's life would be the last four years of my mother's life.

Cancer took my grandmother at 50 years of age, and now cancer was doing the same to my mother at 50 years of age. It was three months from diagnosis to departure. Three months of praying prayers like her life depended upon them. Three months of us refusing this sickness to be unto death. We brought her home in time for Christmas and set up a medical bed in the family room so we could be with her 24/7.

My dad had a yearly Christmas tradition of buying her a single piece of fine jewelry. This year, my mom was looking through a holiday catalog from a local jeweler. She had two pieces picked out and asked me to make her decision for her this year. One of the pieces was a sizable, deep violet tear-shaped amethyst pendant—super elegant and super purple. She and I had four years of faith, believing those words God gave her about my husband. We shared four years of glancing upon the reminder at my desk, springtime violets popping up in our yard, and sharing every purple "coincidence" we came across, encouraging us at just the right time in the oddest places to remember: "There will be a man who hears My voice." The purple pendant was the obvious choice, it was a prophetic pendant declaring that we will see His words come to pass! Nineteen days after the new year started, I lost my mom, and I inherited her pendant. I couldn't help but wonder at times throughout her last days if she didn't have that inheritance in mind all along.

Shortly after she passed, my daughter and I got our first chance to get a place of our own, allowing us to stay close by for my dad. Money was so tight that I was afraid to go. My dad caught me in my tears one night and made a point to let me know I could do it, and everything would be fine. He was right. Everything would be okay because he would always be making sure of it. In turn, we would always go over on Saturdays to get in some grandpa playtime and watch a ball game or a NASCAR race with him.

We moved into a second-floor apartment, apartment number seven, cheap for the prestigious area developing around it. We had two bedrooms, a toy room, and five pieces of furniture: two beds, two dressers, and one butterfly chair. On our first night, we had pizza, Indian style, cross-legged on the floor with napkins. Our home slowly filled out with each rummage sale treasure we'd bring home on the weekends. Money was so tight that I often wondered if moving out was the right thing to do. I remember one particular spring morning, walking out the front door of our building, when a flash of purple below my feet caught my eye. I stopped to look down, and a bundle of wild violets was growing at the foot of the rock bed, landscaping our building right at the door. Every going in and coming out, I was greeted by these violets. His promise did not leave with my mother. It was not just her promise for me but my promise for me. I knew that I was in the right place at the right time for the right reasons. It was my turn to take what my mom knew about God and know Him for myself.

It was in this first home that God had set up a honeymoon suite of sorts. It was where I undressed out of a lot of pain and disappointment, starting with my mom's death, diving into my father's alcoholism, and my lifelong self-pities. It's where I trusted God to father my daughter, to supply all our needs, and continued to grow in my own experiences of hearing Him for myself.

While still living with my parents, a particular man had caught my mom's interest for me, along with a couple of her friends, as a possible husband for me. I had been attending a small group at his sister's and thought that might be a "sign" of him being someone God would have for me. We all did a lot of praying, wondering, and waiting. They would all encourage me to go to events where he would be. He was stylish in a nerdy, artistic way. He was an artist and had a solid career in graphic design. His family was ideal, with the sweetest parents. The only problem was that he showed no interest in me, not one cent. We all assumed he was just "not getting it" and prayed that way for a couple of years. By the time my mom was gone and I was on my own, I remember feeling so desperate for something to happen, just SOMETHING that I determined in my own heart to do something myself.

I was looking out of my second-floor picture window and told God exactly how I thought this should go, and if He wasn't going to say anything after all this time, then I was going to make a move myself. If ever I heard a thundering voice from Heaven, I heard it that day in my heart: "If you go, you go without Me." That statement ripped to my core, the center of my being, where my love for Him could not be denied. I dropped to my knees, sobbed, and thought, "I love You too much ever to go anywhere You will not go." While I was looking for His promised love, He was busy making me His purposed love. All the while He was healing me, I was falling in love with Him first. From that day forward, it would never be possible for me to love a man He didn't give me. I was done "rending the Heavens" for God to do what He already said He would do; I would wait. I would follow Him whole heartedly into the romantic. I got up and told Him, "I don't want to make my own choice. I want Your choice, and I want you to bring him to my door if necessary. I'm not going to go looking for him."

SCENE SIX:

RIVETHEAD

- G -
Exhausted and Fuming

THE FIRST TIME I SET foot inside an automobile manufacturing facility was the same day the company employed me. The building was absolutely massive, and I had gotten lost in it more than once. I had no idea what I was getting into, but it wouldn't take long to find out. As I settled into this type of work routine, I thought, "I'll do this for a little while, but there is no way I can handle it for very long. Everything was just too demanding; it consumed too much of daily life." This would be another prime example of Gary getting to eat his words! I was in for quite a ride in the world of factory life. I was officially a Rivethead. I thought, "A year or two at the most is what I'll devote to this job, with plans to return to Chicago after that." In reality, I was still attempting to plan my own life, you know, that helping God out kind of gig. Yeah, that just doesn't work. So, how long would my employment last at the grand old auto facility?

Things didn't start out so well at the beginning of this auto gig. It was a rough ride for the first few years. I was stuck on 2nd shift with no way out; overtime was mandatory. I had recently moved into a small house on the East side of my home city in a not-so-good neighborhood. My daily commute was 52 miles one way. All this compiled meant one thing: I no longer had a life for myself; I lived to work.

I assumed I would start another band with hopes that this next one would break through, but I found that the music had all but vanished. All doors were closed, which was frustrating. I felt like a mere slave to this nonsensical job. There was nothing that I liked about it. This employment felt like it was robbing me of everything I thought I should be doing. After many months of feeling this apparent thievery, I grew very angry and was always on edge. I was not a pleasant human to be around during this time. It appeared God had all but forgotten about me. I began to search for a way out of this job. I wanted to return to Chicago and made plans to do so. However, those plans went nowhere. Then, for the next couple of years, I searched for anything to better myself as a means to get out. Again, nothing worked. It took well over three years of this striving before I finally grasped that the Lord had cornered me and was not letting me out. Even though I did not understand all that He was up to, I finally gave up all attempts at escaping and agreed to remain as long as He wanted me there. It was then that sweet peace returned. I had missed it so.

You know, basic human nature works hard to be in control and call our own shots, even as Christians. As I observed many peers who seemed to do as they pleased and all would turn out as they wished, it just didn't work for me, even though I tried repeatedly. If I demanded my own plan out of full-on defiance, God would eventually let me have it, but to my detriment. I observed other Christians who made decisions based on nothing more than what they wanted for themselves. I tried that and found it never got me what I thought I wanted. What it delivered was hollow, void of any real substance. It was simply better to do things God's way, even when life got difficult. I finally realized that those people's lives were none of my business. I would deal with my own affairs. At this point of surrender, I saw Him meet me in ways that only He could. Yes, my current circumstances still sucked, but He was in me, and He was with me. God did know what He was up to. He really did care. I began to trust Him more and more through every challenge that came my way. Much spiritual growth was beginning to take place in this long season.

Lessons were still waiting to be learned here, more than the auto manufacturing kind. Early on, when my employment began, I met an adorable dark-haired girl who had expressed an interest in me. For the first time in my life, I stopped and prayed to know if this was His plan *before* I pursued her. Progress! I was beginning to grasp what the Almighty was teaching me in the Romantic space.

There was no immediate answer, so I paused. And this time, I would wait until God revealed it to me one way or another. Am I glad that I waited? You better know it! Eventually, He pulled back the curtain enough so I could see what I did not see at first: this cutie was a bit of a player. There was more there than met the eye. What a disaster it would have been if I had entered a romance with this girl. Warning! Avoid at all costs. Major lesson learned: pray before chasing. But I was hardly through with the divine education.

God has an opinion on this romantic stuff. He has more to say on the matter than most of us realize. He wants more from us than just to call on Him to clean up our mess. How about we stop making the messes, huh? I was intrigued. But where do I go now?

My confidence in His romantic ways had come to the point where I began to sense the Almighty moving me to let go of the traditional American idea of dating. I couldn't articulate what it was, but I knew something fundamental about it wasn't quite right. All Jesus was saying at this point was, "All I want you to do is trust Me." That's it? It spooked me. How will anything happen if I don't help? And He said again, "Do you trust Me?" Uh, maybe?

More relational circumstances would be coming that were meant to assist me in better understanding His ways in the romantic. One evening, the strangest thing happened at a Bible study. An older man approached me and asked if I would be interested in his daughter (romantically). What? Did we go back in time? How old school was this? Regardless, a thought hit me: What if Heaven was arranging this?

Perhaps I needed to take some initiative and explore it further. Sometime later, I asked this man if he thought his daughter would like to join a group of us on a ski trip. A gross look washed over his face, "No, forget it." He replied point blank. This didn't even seem like the same dude who was very open and friendly before. What had just happened? I was perplexed. I was also angry. Why? It wasn't that I had hung my hat on this girl; my heart wasn't shattered over the experience; I was full of anger that NOTHING ever worked out for me in the world of the romantic. It just did not make sense. But in the aftermath, quite a revelation was coming my way!

Due to the strange way this invitation came about, I had convinced myself that this man's daughter had to be an invitation from God because he was a church leader. The truth was I didn't know for sure. When this latest "possibility" tanked like so many before, it would be my final effort to assist God with making a match of the romantic kind.

That evening, as I climbed into bed, I'd had enough of all the failures. I was exhausted and fuming. By now, I was in my mid-thirties, watching all my peers marry whom they wished. They did it with ease while absolutely nothing was ever happening for me. My romantic history was full of everything I had attempted on my own and ended with me not getting who I wanted and getting a series of broken hearts instead.

Frustration led to anger, and I was boiling over with it. I understood that God cared about the romantic, but where was He? And with one of the ugliest displays of honesty before the throne of Heaven, I began to vent to Him. It was candid and ghastly. Words that don't need to be repeated were spoken. This went on for an hour or so until I was empty. Jesus had heard it all. He did not retaliate, nor was He shocked at what I had brought to the throne. I lay there quietly and whispered, "Do you have anything to say to me?" In that quietness, I heard a whisper directing me to grab a pen and find some paper. Did He have anything to say? Did He ever!

It came not from my mind but from a deeper place of just knowing. They were wonderful words without being audibly spoken. "Do you not see that nothing has worked because I have been guarding and protecting you? Are you aware that you have been hidden? For I must say no to everything that is not for your best so that I can say yes to what is best. I must tell you no many times in order to tell you yes once. It is I who have chosen your wife. She will be like no other to you. She is a gift that can only be given by Me. Stop trying to find for yourself what only I can give you. She is not in this period of your life; she will be found in the next. Look around—this house, your job; these are temporary and tied to your singleness. When these things come to an end, she will be found because I will present her to you. All I ask of you is to believe Me and rest."

What a shift in the atmosphere. Such tranquility! Utter peace. Complete rest fell upon me. I lay there with tears and worshiped the Almighty. He's so brilliant! There is nothing like being a man in God's presence and hearing His voice and His will for your life. I was never so grateful to know I am never alone, never without Him.

So that night, for me, the American idea of dating, with its searching and striving, met its final death. This cultural idea may be helpful if I wanted just any girl I could find for myself, but if I wanted the gift from the Heavens, guessing through dating was unnecessary. It only proved to spoil, frustrate, and ruin things.

This experience with God lit a fire in me to look deeply at the original plan of how God still wanted to direct romance. I'd heard many tales of humans crediting Heaven for all sorts of love. I knew many of these were nothing but a facade, an imposter of the real thing! The only way to get to the truth was to comb through the Holy Bible and see the fingerprint of the Divine in various love stories. My favorite is the first one, Adam and Eve. I saw in their story that love was meant to be a gift from God and not something I had to strive to find for myself.

This was not a task accomplished in a few months. Little did I know it was going to take me many years. During this time of study, I finally saw the wisdom of God cornering me into a job that isolated me for a greater work He would eventually call me into. It would demand the great attention this kind of isolation would provide. This time of being set apart was so I could "discover" how the Creator always meant for romantic love to happen. I had to purposely forget everything the culture, peers, and even the American church taught me about the romantic. Purposed to forget everything I already knew and start over, I allowed God Himself to teach me.

This experience would become my call, and my purpose to communicate. I read, dug, studied, and took endless notes, filling entire notebooks. I observed people in everyday life and how they did love. I could see a vast difference between those Christian couples who matched themselves and those who believed God to match them. I heard the Spirit whisper insights and truths to me. Sometimes, you could find me scouring the bookshelves of Christian literature for any resources that may offer help. I was on a mission!

If I could write a concluding statement from my discovery this season, it would be: "What God originally intended in His plan for romantic love and what American culture practices is not the same. My mission was clear; I had to share how incredible God's ways in the romantic can be!

SCENE SEVEN:

ELLIOT

- G -

Why Not Me?

WITH ENDURING INTENSE STUDY comes life-altering radical change. Several years had passed since I first buried my nose in the Book of Books, seeking truth on this love thing. Though I could spear someone through with renewed answers on the romantic. Something vital was missing. I was about to discover that all this new truth would be tested. Could it be trusted? Will it hold up in real life? Can it stand up under severe pressure? It's one thing to cruise along in belief when there is no one on the "love horizon" and another thing to prove those beliefs while under the fire of serious consideration and the possibility of an opportunity that looks so good to you. I was on the brink of the darkest nine months of my life.

A young lady named Holly showed up at a meeting of believers I attended on Monday nights. A new person, there was nothing unusual about that, and I gave this no special attention. But circumstances later aligned through a couple of activities I was involved in, and I spent some time one-on-one with her. Neither of us sought this out. Holly was very outgoing, and she loved to serve others. This extended time with her made me wonder if Jesus was up to something here. I began to ask Him if this was so. Could she be more than a friend? Was she the one? I had my belly full of self-attempts to help God. I quickly received an answer but not the one I had hoped for; He simply said what I had heard Him say so often—wait. My reply? Wait again? Man, Jesus knows already; why can't He just say one way or the other? It was not the super spiritual answer I wanted, but I waited nonetheless.

I cared for Holly had an interest in her, and had a natural love for her that was not romantic. It was then that all sorts of trouble started. Wicked enemies (spiritual) came on the scene and began to harass and torment me in connection to Holly. They pressured me to pursue her and jump ahead of the Lord. This was an element that I never expected. Daily, I heard obsessive thoughts and felt hopeless gloom. This was a very strange and dark season. What was it like? I would hear Holly's name in my thoughts during the day, like someone was chanting her name over and over. This was an obsessive element. Then, I felt a deep sadness mimicking a broken heart. At first, it was difficult to pinpoint where this madness was coming from. I liked Holly and enjoyed her company, but I was certainly not in love with her. There was no reason for a broken heart. Was I losing my mind? My appetite vanished, I didn't eat much, and I lost significant weight. Much time was spent praying, hours a day. I also shared this with some trusted friends who prayed with me. There would be moments of clarity, but nothing I did would cause it to lift. I had never experienced anything of the like before.

Holly herself had no idea what I was going through. Truthfully, I just wanted to run from the entire ordeal; no girl was worth this sort of anguish. But I couldn't. Why, you might ask? The answer Jesus gave me was to wait. It wasn't yes, and neither was it no. If Holly was indeed His plan for me later and I had run, I wouldn't have been in the right position. Wait meant that I had to remain until further light presented itself. This taught me that there was something to glean in the process, no matter how it was to end up. In many situations, it is perfectly normal and right not to know either way for a period. The only resolution was to wait for God to say more.

I battled this continually, struggling to keep my soundness of mind. It took some time, but it was eventually understood that the source of this mess was pure wicked in origin. I had been a little bit crazy over girls in the past due to my adolescence, but this was beyond human obsession. This was demonic intimidation. Sounds strange, I know. After many months, bit by bit, this darkness finally began to subside. As difficult as it was, I remained under this tension until Jesus revealed that Holly would only be a great friend for a season. The freedom I was beginning to experience felt sweet.

So what on God's big blue marble was this all about? In time, a few things became clear. The first is that devils were applying severe pressure on me to throw caution to the wind and pursue Holly without God's directive. In other words, get ahead of the divine plan. I believe that if I had done so, she would have agreed. A few times, she clearly left herself open for me to chase her. In retrospect, Holly could have made a good wife, but that wasn't enough. I wanted and needed Heaven's choice in a wife; none other would do. Pursuing Holly outside of God's desire would be settling for Holly. I would ruin the purpose that God had ahead for us both. The wicked liars were well aware of that and offered me a decoy, a compromise with heavy pressure.

The second takeaway was that God allowed the fire to test if this newfound revelation of His plan for the romantic worked. It's one thing to have studied this stuff, but let's see if it will hold up in this world I live in every day. You see, before the Almighty grants you a gift in saying yes to the right person, He must first say no to all the others. And even more, the Almighty must teach us to say no to ourselves. Can I say no to an appealing and attractive girl when God has said nothing yet? Could I stand under that weight with the added fire from hell spitting at me and hold my ground until Jesus gives a clear yes or no answer? By the sheer grace of God, I did just that. This experience would be the test of all tests. Nothing else I would ever endure in the divine romance business would compare to that initial trial.

And thirdly, God wanted to shift my direction radically. Although I was not in evident rebellion, I found myself in a place of contentment and comfort where nothing in me would have changed if the Lord had not interrupted my thoughts with His own. The best way to describe it was drifting. I was floating along in whatever way the wind blew. Something radical had to come and shake me out of this ease so I would see the need to change course. I needed to point my arrow to something specific. A difficulty of sorts was required to get my attention. God allowed some kind of "storm" to jolt me out of my lazy thinking. This hardship did its job. It eventually brought me to where I am now, bringing the good news of the God of the romantic.

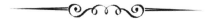

I believed it was time to find a new church to plug into. A long search didn't appeal, so I simply asked Jesus where He wanted me. I was invited to church during a phone conversation with a neighbor. It was one of the larger assemblies in the city. I found a large and tight group of singles and fit into them well, even though I was one of the oldest in the group. Eventually, I found a new best friend there. I'd only had a few times where my best friend was a female. Her name was Allison, and she was a breath of fresh air. She, too, understood this God-given love thing, and we were both drawn into friendship because of it. We would sit for long spells and sharpen each other's convictions.

I had been commissioned to teach a Bible class for a few weeks. Most in attendance were singles. The obvious topic for me would be Heaven-ordained relationships. This was a perfect opportunity to learn to communicate everything I had been given. Allison agreed to help me with an outline. Amid our work one evening, she listened to the substance I had to offer and bluntly declared, "You need to write a book!" Me? Write a book? You can't be serious? Other than song lyrics, I had not attempted to write anything "serious" since high school. I told Allison that I didn't have a clue how even to begin, but she replied that she did and generously offered to walk me through it. As I pondered that thought for the next few days, this question kept haunting me: "Why not me?" I began to grasp the fact that I had been through a lot of testing and a lot of study, not only for my sake but for the good of others as well. A book now made sense and a book it would be!

Off I went. Most of my spare time was spent on this newfound assignment. At first, I struggled to find enough solid substance to fill a couple of hundred pages, so I began writing relatable stories that would apply to the subject. Those stories became long-winded in an attempt to make a legit read. After many months, it was finally finished. I dropped it on Allison's desk with a sigh of relief. I really did it; I wrote a book! Then we began to read it together. After several nights, when the last sentence was read, one word came to mind—RUBBISH. It was awful and fully deserved that one-word assessment. There was no way I could call that my book with my name on the cover. But it was a great learning experience, and only one thing could have been done: I told Allison I would rewrite it.

Sitting at my little desk with my laptop glowing, I did what I should have done before: I prayed. "God, if this is what You would have me to do, I need You in this. Others have written similar things to what You've shown me, and I don't want to simply duplicate their work. Let this book be what You would have me say. Make it unique, make it mine —Yours and mine." And you know what? I'm elated to relay that's exactly what He did! The Scriptures began to explode with hidden insights I hadn't seen before. And those notebooks that I had filled with personal revelation? Much substance was gleaned from these as well.

When the new version was dropped on Allison's desk this time, I knew we had something for real! Although I wanted people to read it, the reality is that I didn't know what to do with it. The publishing world was foreign territory to me. So, I had copies of the manuscript printed and bound with rings to give away to anyone interested, and I thought it would speak to them. I did this for years, giving away hundreds and hundreds of copies. Sometime later, I did some serious edits and had the book professionally printed and bound with spiral rings in a legit book size. Many of these were sold at speaking events, and eventually, many were also given away.

When the book got a more professional look, I also decided to use a professional name, which the industry calls a pen name. Authors and entertainers do it all the time. My birth name comes from Czechoslovakia, as my father's parents were immigrant children. Our name is hard to pronounce and spell. The last thing I wanted was to cause potential readers to trip over it. I chose Elliot. Author Elisabeth Elliot was the very first and most influential author and speaker on all things romantic from a divine perspective. I would listen to her speak on the radio and knew that I knew I was in good company. I chose to pay tribute to all I had gleaned from her and adopted the Elliot name as my own. Besides, Elliot looks good on book covers!

As I write this, I sit in what Kim and I call our "Lava Lounge." It's the other side of our dining room, which is illuminated with a slew of lava lamps. Laying on the top shelf of our tall bookcase are two books, *God of the Romantic* and *Veiled Unto His Pleasure*. The first is my final version of the original work I had begun over 20 years ago with my friend Allison. It is legitimately published this time! There have been many changes since I first wrote it single and waiting. It now has a new chapter at the end. It tells how God fulfilled the very words He spoke to me that night I lay angry in bed all those years ago. The wife He sent is the author of the second book. She is an outstanding writer herself. Like me, she calls all of us to know Jesus as she did in the world of the romantic. God doesn't just match personalities. He matches purposes!

It was almost as if I was speaking to a stranger, but she had something "prophetic" to deliver that I wasn't expecting. The longer I watched her, the more I could see my mother in her. My parents and I were in Virginia, Mom's home state. Across the way in the tiny living room was my grandmother, whom I had not seen in 23 years. I never really knew any of my grandparents; my father's parents were deceased before I was born, and my mother's father passed away when I was six. Her mother, Marie, had been the only surviving grandparent, and I had only seen her around five times over the years. Now she was very old, and her health wasn't the best. I was now 38. I had heard the tales that she was one feisty firecracker if there ever was one! Her age had done nothing to diminish that.

My mother was one of eight siblings. As we sat, stories began to spin on the eight of them as they were growing up in the mountains. The drama was in full supply. Things then progressed to the current day. This one fighting with that one, he doesn't get along with her, that one isn't speaking to the others, holy cow! One thing I've always respected about my Ma, she steered clear of all these family squabbles. She would not play and was very private. Her brothers and sisters shared their dirty laundry with the world, but not my dear mother.

Soon, the conversation moved to the sticky subject of divorce. I watched as my grandmother displayed a sad countenance over the fidelity of her children. Divorce that wreaked havoc on their lives was thick in my mother's family. So much cheating, so much pain. Marriage, infidelity, splits, remarriage, more infidelity, and more splits. None of them held any kind of discernment in whom they married. It was an open, free-for-all.

My mother was the only member of her entire family who was still married to her original husband. All others had made a mess of themselves. My grandma had a clue that there was something seriously wrong in her children's lives. She respected Mom for tapping into Jesus to make her own marriage work. My grandmother asked me if I had someone special. Before I could speak, Ma interjected that I was waiting on Christ, trusting Him for the right mate. She shared that I had studied the issue for some time and authored a book. My grandmother broke out into a big smile. She knew that the cycle of wrecking your life with toxic romance would be broken with me. Then she spoke these simple but prophetic words, "It's about time someone in this family got it right!" These were some of the last words she spoke to me before she left this life soon afterward.

- K -
Once Upon a Dream

Bekah stood on the platform before us, orchestrating an attempt at giving away the bride at our wedding rehearsal. She was our wedding ceremony coordinator. My daughter, Andee, was my personal bridal coordinator for my wedding day. Andee and her new husband, Zech, ensured we had a timely arrival and clean getaway following our ceremony. Yes, my daughter got married before me. She got a lot of things in life before me. Choosing life has proven to be a multiplier of many good things. Both girls took care of every hiccup in between, making our experience purely seamless.

Bekah was around 15 when we first met. I am trying to remember ever having an official introduction. My daughter was only about seven then, and I would cross paths with Bekah at church. Bekah had an essence of effervescent purity about her, unmatched by any other pre-teen around us. I had just finished a book that secured me so tightly into faith, believing God could match me with a husband and that He wanted to. There was something about Bekah's purity of heart that I wanted to help preserve, so I bought a copy for her and handed it to her in the hallway of our church as our youth group was letting out. I can't remember how I came to know her well enough to feel that liberty, but now, here she is at my wedding, married to her first love, mother of five, directing my wedding ceremony. The book I shared that day was called *Passion and Purity* by Elisabeth Elliot. While Gary was instituting her surname as his pen name, I, too, was experiencing a romantic transformation through her writings.

Focus on the Family was a popular radio program in the 90s. As a single mom, I could use all the parenting wisdom I could find. One day, I heard this soft-spoken yet assertive older lady speak of her love for

Jesus in the most abandoned ways. She shared about pressing into Christ to know His pleasures regarding a young love interest on campus. It sounded like we knew the same Jesus. The first time I read *Passion and Purity*, I was blown away by more than the evidence of a divine match set up by God. I was blown away at her passionate devotion to Him, God, her Creator. The book played out their chance meeting and the slow revelation of their future coming together while fighting the temptation to get ahead of her love and to get ahead of her God. Her submission to the desires of God's heart over her own was unbelievable to me. At one point, so overwhelmed by it, I put it down and said to myself, "Who does that?" Who denies their feelings and their desires like that? It seemed so unnatural to me. In fact, it was unnatural; it was supernatural. As much as I was fascinated by her relationship with God, I found it equally unbelievable.

Soon, I began to search the Bible for love stories. I looked for principles in dating and knowing how to find one person God would be pleased for me to marry. I found three stories: Adam and Eve, Issac and Rebekah, and Boaz and Ruth. All three men were busy working. All three ladies were prepared and presented. No dating to be seen. It seemed so unnatural. It was. It was much like Elizabeth's experience, it was supernatural.

About seven years into this promise God made me, I was concerned I may be missing Him. Maybe I needed to be doing something to help Him out. Each of these women, Elisabeth Elliot, Eve, Rebekah, and Ruth, were women dedicated to God and His will over their own. They knew Him and trusted Him in ways I wanted to. I was able to conclude in full faith that I did not need to help Him any more than they did. I needed to trust Him like they did, which meant I needed to know Him like they did. I was learning that this new life in Christ was about knowing Him. My whole life is about knowing Him single, as a mother, as a daughter, and one day through being a wife. A new sense of peace settled deep inside, and for the first time, I was absolutely convinced my wedding day was on the calendar. I remember taking my increased faith in His promise and kneeling over my borrowed couch in apartment number seven, telling Him I trusted Him even more, and with trembling in my soul, I gave Him my singleness to do with it what He wanted until He saw it was time for me to marry.

He inspired me to start a small group out of my church for young girls called Girl Talk. We gathered every other week to be girls, talk about boys, the desires of our hearts to be loved, and how God truly saw us in all of that. I desired everyone to fall in love with Jesus while waiting for the one to whom God desired to give them away to. Bekah was the first girl to come and sit at my feet while my daughter, seven years younger, peeked around the corner of her bedroom, overhearing through all the giggles the wisdom and love I had come into with Christ. Over the years, Bekah and my daughter remained my biggest fans and longest students. Of course, my daughter was more like a captive of mine. All those years, I was doing my part to help them be prepared to be given away; they were now both preparing me to be given away on my wedding day, and I felt the reward of my long-lived faith all the more.

Waiting was not easy. It's not supposed to be. It's one of the most crucifying elements of faith. Every doubt and accusation against God you don't think you have comes to the surface for an ugly fight. I always had two choices: harden my heart and keep my lies or surrender them and get more truth. And God knows what He's doing when He gives you a promise. He enchants you with more than you can imagine, and your love for Him abounds every time He brings it up. Just when you think you can't wait any longer and you're caught up in your insecurities, God reminds you of the last thing He said about your promise. Once you surrender, He brings the promise up again, and it only gets bigger. At least, that's how it rolled for me.

I had a moment of coughing up my complaints and surrendering them to God, after which He brought His promise up to me again. This time, it was in a dream. In the dream, I was standing in front of a local college frat house where I had partied back in the day. I had strong inner compulsions convincing me that my promised husband was in that house. I walked into the front door, convinced I would find him. When I opened the front door, there was nothing before me but a white hall of closed doors. I opened the first door, and to my disgust, I saw a room full of naked men and women performing all kinds of perversions in an intoxicated state. I could barely stand the sight of the debauchery and quickly slammed the door. I checked the next door. It was the same seedy scene. The third door was also the same.

I was dumbfounded, knowing my husband was in this house. I took the stairs to the second floor. As I turned the corner of the top stairs, it was another white hall of closed doors. You guessed it. I opened another door of disgust. I knew that I knew he wouldn't be on this floor either, so I stopped opening doors. At the end of the hall was a tiny door like something you'd see in *Alice in Wonderland*. I walked up toward it, opened it, and bent down to walk through it. I carefully walked up an unfinished staircase to a dimly lit attic. When I reached the top, I encountered a profound presence of peace, like when entering an ancient sanctuary. I slowly turned to the left to see a man with long hair sitting in a wooden chair, head bowed in sleep, with a Bible lying open across his lap. I turned to the right to see a bed dressed with a 1950s white chenille bedspread completely undisturbed.

Two things I knew immediately: This man was my husband, and I was to lay upon the foot of his bed and wait for him to awaken and claim me as his own. It was as if the love story in the book of Ruth played itself out in some sweet way fitted for me. When I awoke, I heard God in my heart say, "You ask where your husband is. I tell you, I have Him hidden in Christ like you." I was humbled to my core to understand that the reason I had no one showing interest in me was because I was hidden, veiled in a sense, being saved away for this man and him for me.

.

It helped me to realize my husband was tucked away, knowing Christ in this same way: through promise and waiting. One thing I had a hard time believing was his long hair. I mean, guys with long hair in bands were a long-time desire of mine, and for my husband to have long hair sounded too good to be true, as though God had no interest in what I had desired. He interrupted my irrational reasoning: "He will be your heart's desire." What a good Father! Still thinking actual rock-star long hair was too good to be true, I modified His words to be only a metaphor for desire. I settled for the idea I could easily trust; I will desire whom God desires for me, long hair or not.

God's Word encouraged me to seek Him first, and all "these things" will be added to me. I knew every day was another day closer, and every day had the potential to grow me into the wife that was being promised to my husband. Every day, I lived out what was reasonable and what was possible. Still, eventually, the status quo lifestyle would press in on my heart like a heavy burden to be an unacceptable lifestyle. The ordinary pushed me to question whether there was more to life.

This new compulsion for more than the ordinary drove me to learn about how I was gifted, challenged me to question why I was born, and increased my intolerance for the "same ol same ol." About this time my job wanted to transfer me to another city too far away from my daughter's school. I was taught to follow job security, but I just couldn't. I started a new job to avoid the commute. I was miserable. The new job was just more of the same nothingness.

I was very successful in my training and dying to run away from it at the same time. This is what being a single mom left alone to make decisions according to responsibilities instead of faith gets you. The most drastic thing I could think of doing with my anguish was to burn up my lunch hours in our church's prayer room. Daily, I skipped lunch, got on my knees in the prayer room, knowing there had to be more to this life with Jesus, and begged God to push me into my destiny. Three months later, I was fired! I was fired from my mind-numbing job even though I was doing everything well, confirmed by a raise one month earlier. My boss had no reasonable explanation for this decision except, "This just isn't working." As he spoke, I saw his hardened heart as the answer to my many prayers in the prayer room. I had no idea where I was heading or how I would provide for my daughter, but I knew one thing: This was the beginning of God pushing me into my greater purposes.

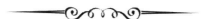

When I gaze at Andee and Bekah, I see my life in Christ, my hard, weird, scary, thrilling, enchanting life in Christ worth the "yes." I had a couple of "words from the Lord," a couple of dreams of my future husband tucked away in what is now decades of a single life lived with Christ. It was not a lot, but it was enough. There were a zillion confirmations that I was moving in the right direction and a zillion reasons to quit. For much of my life, I had this profound question looping in the background of my mind: What's the point? What was the point of my life? What was the point of life, period? Why was it so hard for me?

The Lord of the Rings was a staple film trilogy during my season of singleness. Upon the first watch, I was overwhelmed by the fainting emotions that arose when the impossible presented itself in the film. I mean, a handful of Hobbits facing a zillion nasty Orcs, who wouldn't faint or quit or both? By the third year of my annual winter solace viewing, God came near and asked me what was different about watching the film this time around. I told Him I did not know. He replied, "You are no longer overwhelmed enough to quit when the impossible is portrayed." He was right! Waiting on a dream, decades of believing despite what I was seeing and feeling, worked to kill the quitter in me. His ways are not our ways, and that scripture could serve as a warning for the faint of heart. Like, "Get ready; He's about to blow your mind with what He can do through you!" His ways to love are better than our ways. It's a good thing I was taking notes all along the way, never thinking I would be writing about this life for the sake of others.

It never crossed my mind that I would be an author someday. But that idea of being an artist with words really fits the creative image I had of myself back in high school: that cool girl with the black t-shirt, DIY bleached torn jeans, and Chuck Taylors, living in a city-size loft apartment with a high ceiling and exposed brick walls. Only God knows how to take an original desire and make it holy with Himself and His plans to see us fulfilled in who He originally created us to be.

SCENE EIGHT

REVELATION CALLING

- G -
Dark and Theatrical

I T DIDN'T MAKE SENSE TO me. Obvious to you by now, one of the greatest joys in all of life for me was music. I was both a massive fan and consumer, but the biggest kick, the greatest thrill, was playing and creating music. My existence had been forever changed when I first slung that precision bass over my shoulder during my high school years. And now...it seemed to be gone. Not long ago, I was standing under stage lights before rowdy crowds with my autographed limited edition Jackson Super Strat, giving it all I had. Since factory life had taken over and eaten up life, my guitars remained dormant, buried in their hard shells. They were collecting dust.

I tried to join other bands and attempted to start new bands, but nothing found teeth; everything fizzled out. It was a heavy source of frustration for me. It truly felt as if this vital part of me had died. Music, at this point, was now just something delegated to consumption. I was too much of a fan to allow it to completely disappear so I could still be found at rock shows whenever the opportunity presented itself.

Though Metal was and continues to this day to be my preference, I also indulged in many other genres at my discretion. Nothing is quite as intimate as an acoustic performance in a small venue. And I would take in a local classic rock cover act. There were some good ones in town at the time. A more recent radical pastime, I discovered, was dancing to hardcore industrial tunes, synth-pop, or darkwave by a disc jockey or a live band! One of the more unlikely shows I participated in this season was Christian artist Nicole C. Mullen, who is all about urban pop. What was unusual was that this particular concert was at a sprawling church in small-town Illinois, somewhere you would never think to find such gritty dance swagger and song. The sanctuary was nearly full of farmer types doing their best to imitate big city grooves. I know Nicole had to smile at all these white people trying their hardest, but she treated them with love anyway. And yep, I had a great time myself.

One of my other "escapes" was revisiting my childhood by playing baseball. One afternoon, while crushing yellow rubber balls at a batting cage, someone informed me that the city had an adult baseball league. This was a fact I never knew. Man, I hadn't played actual baseball since high school! I would be strapping on my catcher's gear the following season during many summer evenings. The experience made me feel like a kid again, reliving Little League. I lived for baseball during those adolescent years. As for now, baseball was a pleasant relief from the routine and everyday drudgery of factory life. It gave me something to stay busy with. After several years of hitting the dusty diamond, late spring had arrived again, and it was time to lace up the cleats to prepare for the upcoming season. I went to only one practice, and something wasn't quite right this year. I sensed a hesitation of sorts. As much as I loved baseball, I really didn't want to be there this time. What was happening? I didn't quite know at the time. But that day, I walked away from the diamond, never to return. I had played my last game that past September in a tournament. I was now 40 years old.

My employment experience could have been more enjoyable, but understanding it was for my good now, I had learned to be content. I had stopped striving to get out of it. All I desired now was to complete what God had given me to do. I was in it for the long haul.

Years passed as I settled into a lifestyle of studying and writing when music finally moved back into my life little by little. In the past, I had been used to signing autographs, people wanting group pictures, and being a big deal, and now, no one knew me in that context. This initial return to music for public performance was strumming acoustic for a couple of friends as they sang Christmas favorites in a local bookstore. It was a humbling experience, but I was thrilled to be playing. It didn't stop there. We did some coffeehouse gigs after that, and though it was far from my metal past, it was enjoyed nonetheless. Soon, a youth pastor at my church commissioned me to assemble a band for the youth services on Sunday nights. That brought me closer to the kind of thing that I really desired. That gig lasted a year or so for me. Then, one of the most radical musical endeavors I had ever participated in presented itself: Christian Goth. Yes, it is a real thing.

A great friend I had known for years opened an all-ages club/ church dedicated to the underground subculture. I played guitar for his band. It was loud, dark and very theatrical, and I loved it! We could be found in heavy makeup, wearing six-inch heeled boots, and dressed in a lot of black. We used movie clips with performance art and live music during the shows. It was a multimedia experience unlike anything I had ever seen Christians attempt. And if that wasn't enough, out of the group of these like-minded believers, I joined a second band that played hypnotic blends of heavy rock and electronic dance. This show was accompanied by high-energy original video clips. Both bands were fully unique in the Christian community, with no one doing anything like it. I had always admired the leaders of each of these bands for presenting musical art that stood on its own merits. These would prove to be extremely influential for me in the future. Just when I thought music opportunities had exited, it returned, and this time for reasons I had yet to imagine.

It was a Tuesday, much like any other. I was about my daily duties at the car plant, and I was singing to myself. I was about to have an unexpected visitation from the Almighty that would change my life.

In the late 80s, my favorite rock band was Seattle Veterans Queensryche. This band was far from the Sunset Strip poodle party type that was everywhere in those days. To be fair, I dug that stuff, too, but Queensryche had things to say in their own way, both musically and visually. In 1988, the band released their epic and pinnacle work, *Operation Mindcrime*. This release is a brilliant piece of art that tells the story of a junkie named Nikki who is manipulated by an evil man, Dr. X. While there is no time to get into the details of this tale here, the story marries the music perfectly. And speaking of the music, to my ears, it's a perfect blend of heaviness and melody, with intelligent guitar riffs for days! The songs resonate in your mind forever. I couldn't put it down for months when I first purchased *Operation Mindcrime*. The band never came close to capturing this level of greatness again. To this day, *Operation Mindcrime* remains my all-time favorite album.

So, that Tuesday at the factory, I sang one of the songs from this epic Queensryche release to myself. I was in a good mood, remembering what a rich experience this record has been for me all these years. Then suddenly, what seemed to come from out of the Heavens, I heard the Spirit of God whisper with bold clarity, "I want you to write and assemble a concept story in song much like Queensryche did. I want you to write about My ways in the romantic realm." This whispering stopped me in my footsteps. All I could do for several minutes was stand there and ponder what I had just heard. Without question, this idea did not originate within me. I had heard this familiar quiet voice before and knew it was the Almighty.

While I had written and recorded songs for years, this was sure to be a daring undertaking. With these words assigning me to my new commission, I could see the brilliance of how God had been working to lead me to this place for decades. There was a reason I was drawn to the overblown theatrics of early Kiss. The tales that Alice Cooper told with his character were another influence. Later, the twisted makeup and production of Marylyn Manson and Ghost would get my attention. The message that some of these acts are not something I would endorse, but I was drawn toward the theatrical and artistic level alone. But it was Queensryche who put a story together with a song that revealed to me how a rock show could communicate much like a movie or play did. It intrigued me to no end. And there were my own experiences of playing in theatrical goth bands that used images and costuming to reveal Jesus unorthodoxly to those in the counterculture. Other Christian musical endeavors like Savior Machine and my friends in White Collar Sideshow all told me this could be done. Eventually, all of these influences would meet in my mind to write and develop my own tale in drama and song, *Escaping Forevermore.*

- K -

I Don't Want a Nice Guy

"Do you know your wealth? More than diamonds sitting on a shelf."
—"Baby Girl" by Nicole C. Mullen

That single lyric could have been a banner over the second half of my life as a single. I, too, remember seeing Nicole C. Mullen live at a very sizable contemporary church off the beaten path of a very rural community. And yes, it was the very same show Gary was at! And no, we did not meet, but the thought of how many times we may have passed one another that evening is trippy! I had not been in a live music environment since my daughter was born nearly 13 years ago. It was unusual that this particular concert was at a sprawling church in small-town Illinois, somewhere you would never think to find such gritty dance swagger and song. The sanctuary was packed. We owned the front row, and I danced so hard that night with my daughter. I felt every word in that song. Not only was the truth rocking me, but the live music atmosphere felt like a homecoming of sorts. It was not my beloved hard rock but it was fun all the same.

Running the roads with my band friends slowed to a serious halt early on. My daughter's worth and my growing relationship with

Jesus drew me into other directions for what my soul and spirit needed most at that time. The church became my new tribe; they were family. As a single mother, I was drawn to families to help fill our gap. I remember being anxious about attending my first parent-teacher conference. I was not as concerned about my daughter's grades as I was about how she was adjusting to the family culture schools naturally bring. When her teacher told me that socially, she showed no lack, I was blessed. I was grateful. I was humbled. Intentionally putting us into whole family relationships within our church was not only helping me, but it was also helping her. And I'd think to myself, "Who knew, maybe my husband would finally show up in one of these groups."

Our time in apartment number seven came to a close. So much healing had taken place there for me, and my greatest reward was the intimacy I experienced in my relationship with Jesus. I was truly hidden in Him and was beginning to prefer it to anything less than His desires for us. We were a power couple. He was my deepest and truest companion. I started to write about it, teach on it, counsel from it, and when the opportunity offered itself, I preached about it. I was understanding my identity in Him, my gifts from Him, and my purpose with Him. I had finally figured out the answer to that relentless question that pestered me, "What's the point?" The point was knowing Him and making Him known (John 17:3).

I thought I also knew my worth, but soon after that concert, what I thought I knew in my heart would be tested to a great degree in real life. There had been no romantic interests to speak of since God first promised me a husband. Once, my pastor, who was also my boss as I administered segments of his ministry, proposed a new guy who started attending our church. His best hook line was, "He's a really nice guy." Without even thinking, I snapped, "I don't want a nice guy." He looked at me like I had a screw loose and said, "What? You want a mean guy?" I knew what he was saying, but it took me a while to understand what I was really saying. Jesus had just invited me to call upon Him with the promise to show me great and mighty things, things not seen by me before, a long season of Him revealing secrets of His heart through mystery (Jeremiah 33:3). He even confirmed it with countless split-second sightings of the number 33 on the clock, scoreboards, road signs, and store receipts. He also began to wake me at 3:33 in the morning to pray with Him. He was inviting me into so much more than a marriage to a nice guy.

I had gone to too many hard places with Christ and overcame, making me desire someone dangerous where faith was concerned. I desired so much more than nice; I desired a man of daring faith, and everything in me could not compromise. I'd rather be single until my death than settle for less than that. My relationship with Christ set the standard for what I desired in a husband: a man on a mission. A man who'd been through the valley of death as many times as it took to know Christ in such a way that he'd be willing to look a fool to the world around him just to help make Him known.

Shortly after that exchange, my girlfriends invited me to a revival service because it was being led by a man who traveled the country, making Christ known through powerful demonstrations of God's presence. He was my age. He was never married. He was attractive in a Hollywood picturesque way. It's hard to believe he was still single until I understood he was also waiting for God's choice. I went to the service. My friends were convinced we'd be a great match like last time. I was quick to dismiss it because it appeared, at first sight, to be too good to be true. I had to leave the service quickly after meeting him to get alone with God. I was overwhelmed with a new revelation; I was grieving His heart with my unbelief over my worth in the face of what appeared too good to be true. I confessed my self-loathing and the denying of His generous nature. Instead, I dared to believe He was that good.

I walked with God for months over that possibility, taking many daring steps of faith, believing He may very well be arranging a match here. I was surrounded by many friends cheering me on, encouraging my understanding, and adding to it. It was like all the stars were finally aligning right up to the day one of my dearest friends asked to meet with me. Fighting back her tears, she revealed that this man was getting married. It came out of nowhere, and the disappointment was almost disabling except for the fact that I was following God and not a man. God said there would be a man who would hear His voice, and this man did not, so I knew God would have something more to say about this.

I remember asking Him one night why He kept encouraging me to present myself to this man through words of encouragement. In my mind's eye, I saw a storefront window with many beautiful crystal vases and one in particular that kept being pushed to the front. He spoke to my spirit, "Because I think you're worth looking at over and over again." For the first time in my life, I agreed. He set up a challenge in my life to believe without seeing fully what He was up to. He walked me into a great crisis of faith, only to come out the other side changed. Mr. Hollywood was not to be my husband, but I was to be changed. I thought I knew my worth before this event, but after this bewildering experience, I came away feeling it. God invited me into a mystery prepared to make me more ready for the husband He had hidden in Christ for me.

Around that time, my dear friend Jeff from the band, my tribe back in the day, had come to Christ, got married, and was leading worship at my church. They were coming into their own faith challenge: church planting. Much of what first appeared to be a young adult ministry was truly meant to be a church started with young adults. Working around old mindsets in our church leadership was quite an obstacle to seeing what we saw. I partnered with them to see their dream realized. We started in their basement and eventually dared to rent some space in a downtown art center two times a month. This art center had a relatively large room on the upper floor where we hired a sound company, put up seating, and assembled a church experience where there was none before. The vibe was edgy and equally cool.

Still single, still waiting, and still wondering, I watched my daughter grow up, and now she was discovering the man she'd soon marry. I remained steadfast in leaning into what God was doing through me and resisting the lies that my dreams had been put on the back burner. I was excited to be a part of the new church plant but sometimes wondered, "What about me and my dreams?" I recalled a pastor once on the radio saying, "When you take care of God's dreams for others, God takes care of your dreams simultaneously." Sometimes, I would secretly question, "Maybe my dream is destined to come true inside their dream?"

ACT II

DID IT HURT WHEN YOU FELL FROM HEAVEN?

SCENE NINE

CHANGE OF SCENERY

- K -
Moving Days

Good, CAN'T YOU JUST GIVE me a job offer this time? Do I have to quit another job without having a job to go to again?" He responded, "Yes, I can give you a job offer this side of Nashville, but then I would not have the pleasure of your faith."

Gary and I were packed and ready to move our newly wedded selves to Nashville, but we did not know where we would be living, let alone where the income to live would be coming from. We were three weeks from our lease ending, and God was asking me to quit my job. I had been in this position before. I didn't like it any more this time than I did the first time. I spent a whole summer waiting to know our next move, only to learn He had revealed it the day I resigned from that job. This time around, I was much more familiar with His ways. Faith first, and understanding will follow.

As the church plant grew, so did my discontent with working for the parent church. I could not see how to move forward from it, and the strain was being felt by the others I served. Additionally, my position would be changing, and I would need to be prepared to make a decision. I planned to take a ten-day retreat to see what God would say.

I spent those days studying God's Word, praying, listening, and worshiping. By day nine, I'm getting mad. I took a significant amount of time away from my daughter, there was a serious transition in employment pending, and my attitude was starting to be heard in my prayers. That morning, I was washing my hair in the bathroom sink. To top off a disheartened week, I got water in my ear. Are you kidding me? I spent all day trying to hear through a clogged ear, throwing my head up and down to get the water to move. I went to bed that night defeated. No heavy-revi, no direction, no new hopes. The morning I was packed up to leave, I stepped down the house's front step, and the water in my ear immediately drained. God said, "There will be an immediate release of what's next when you step down from your job."

Yes! Wait, what? Step down from my job with no job to go to? Gulp. As terrifying as that instruction was, it was equally exhilarating.

I heard! I know what to do, and He will reveal what I need to know once I step out in faith according to what He said. I had a plan. I went back to work on the first of the week and resigned. My pastor was convinced this was right and very supportive of my faith in this. His wife immediately suggested an opening for a ministry in town that I quickly dismissed because I had a much bigger move in mind: Nashville.

You see, two years prior, I met the wife of one of our Nashville pastors, who was super encouraging of me and my dreams. She told me that I could stay with her anytime I was in Nashville. Two months later, an opportunity arose to attend Lou Engle's The Call on 7/7/07 at Nissan Stadium. It was a watershed event for me in many ways. I had a very significant encounter with some college girls who asked me a very uncommon question among Christians but in a very unusual way, "When did you fall in love with Jesus?" To my surprise, I had an answer. I had an interior book of answers, and they came to tears while taking notes of my answer. I understood that day that I had something of the life of Christ that would feed a generation I had yet to meet. Nashville became a much more intriguing location to me that day. By the end of 2008, I caught an event in Nashville with Pastor Bill Johnson, and I took up that southern hospitality invite to stay with my new pastor friend. As I prepared for that trip, God whispered, "Nashville matters."

I wish I could say that the next trip proved Nashville mattered at that time, but nothing significant took place. I spent the summer that followed resigning from my job, striving to get back there. Everything that made sense to me about a move to Nashville never materialized. Within my exasperation and depleting checking account, I surrendered to hear more from God. After all, He said there would be an immediate release of what was next. Where was it? Well, you may have already picked up on it; it was three months back when my pastor's wife *immediately* suggested that local ministry opening I refused to believe. Yep, I missed it, but God knew I'd miss it and kept it for me. Before my bank account emptied, I got a call from the ministry leader with an offer I wanted to refuse but no longer could.

I agreed to be a residing supervisor in a transitional care home for troubled young women. Guess where I took up residence in that home? Right at the top of the narrow staircase leading to an attic bedroom. Sound familiar, like a dream? I thought this "season" of work would finally be where my husband would awake from his slumber in Christ and claim me! My anticipation was high, so I painted that bedroom in Wedding White; literally, that was the name of the white paint I picked. Can't say my faith was without works, right?

I had no indications at the time that my husband was waking up yet, but I sure was. This was more of a crucible experience than a dream come true experience. My daughter was residing in the house, too. It was her senior year. Not the one she had imagined for herself. It was difficult for us both not having our own home during the most accomplished year for a high schooler. I had worked three part-time jobs to keep us going while we ate food stocked from the local food bank. We only had one troubled girl the whole time we were there, which was probably God's mercy on the ministry because I was utterly miserable with this divine placement. I've had a couple of episodes in my life that I like to call "divine discontentment." Times in following Christ where you're put into a circumstance that purposely creates pressure to expose true desires of the heart. My awakening in that place proved that as much as I said I wanted to be where God was, my misery was proving that was not true about me. He was there, and I hated it. It was a profoundly humbling encounter, to say the least.

That pressure also revealed a great understanding of whom I was called to serve: dreamers. Up to this point, I was found encouraging young men and women in their dreams, especially young women, in their hopes to marry someday. Often, people would refer girls to me who were broken by life and family. I always found myself coming up short with little to give them. In this ministry home, I saw that my gifts were more fitting to build up a ministry dream than helping heal brokenness. Eventually, my suggestions to this ministry led to hiring a friend with the gifts and the grace to mend broken women. Unfortunately, leadership felt a loss of control as she brought change, and they eventually dismissed her. I felt her heartbreak as if it was my own. I remember asking God, "Why am I here? Why is my heart breaking for my friend so much more than for the troubled girls here?" He replied, "For you to come to know (through this experience) I've made you for the dreamers."

I've learned over the years that the call(s) God adds to our lives develop slowly like a Polaroid picture. When He spoke that to me, I could glance in the rearview mirror of my life and see how true those words already were. Within this, one of the most trying years of my faith, our church plant was growing. We started with a handful in Jeff's living room, then outgrew their newly refinished basement, and we rent out the local arts center once a month so that our friends could invite friends. Being a friend of dreamers, I always had my "antenna" up for bigger and better. During a leisurely DQ run with my daughter and our one resident girl, we came to a stoplight. As we waited, I glanced to the right and saw a "For Rent" sign on the door of an old funeral home in the heart of our little city. I left Jeff, my dreamer friend, a voicemail with the phone number.

Once stepping down from that job I could see that residential home had its purposed divine work in my heart. My daughter graduated high school. She had her first love interest that year, which God told me would be coming in her senior year. It turned out he was her only love and is now her husband. That year, she had plans for culinary school at the community college in the fall, and I had gotten a full-time job at a prestigious make-up counter. By October, we were packing up and moving into a new apartment and into a permanent home for our little church plant!

- G -
It Was a Strange Time

It was a strange time. Although I couldn't put a finger on the specifics of what was happening, I could sense a season concluding. When I began this automotive manufacturing gig well over two decades ago, life was volatile, and I was seething. There was so much about the lifestyle of factory work that didn't agree with me, and nothing lit my fuse more than being forced to work the night shift.

It took me a few years to adapt and be at peace with that unorthodox schedule. Previously, I had spent over three years on this gloomy shift before being promoted to working days, where I would remain until now. That was about to change again. Due to an emergency, the company announced it would need a few departments to build extra car bodies to keep up with an unusual demand. The only way that this would work was if it was done after hours, at night. I cringed when hearing this news because my first shift department was included. The list would be posted next week of which employees would be bumped to the night shift. I shuffled into the plant that week and found the official company posting. There it was, just as I feared. I would be the senior employee on the second shift beginning Monday of the following week. It would be dishonest to say I was happy about this, but there was a noticeable difference from the first time this had happened. Gone were the fits of anger I experienced when this awful schedule was forced on me. Learning to trust Jesus in this place all these years told me that I really did believe He knew what He was doing. That belief resulted in much peace.

A facility that usually holds around 2,000 union auto workers during the day is sort of eerie when there are less than a hundred humans to be found in the entire building in the evening. In addition to all the silence, most of the place is also in the dark. That should paint an accurate picture of how different the atmosphere was working at night. After a couple of weeks had passed, we had gotten used to all this murkiness. I had been on a limited workload due to a knee injury, so I was excused from regular duties. I floated by filling in and performing specific tasks where needed. I also carried a radio to communicate with management when needed. I was able to roam to places where others couldn't. The plant was so deserted that I could have strutted around naked in most areas, and no one would have known. (That never happened, in case you are concerned.) All this meant was that I had a lot of freedom, which would turn out to be an asset. Little did I know then that another test with a girl was about to come my way.

Since most employees prefer working during the day, the company paid a premium bonus for those working the night shift. I found myself with extra capital on hand. One evening, I asked Jesus if He had anything to say about this bonus coin. For the life of me, I couldn't think of anything I really wanted to purchase. Do you find that odd? What was the reason for this extra jingle in my jeans? One evening, while walking down a long hallway returning from a trip to the restroom, I received my answer; it both shocked and challenged me. I heard a whisper clearly and precisely that said this money is to be set aside for your wife's wedding ring! Put this extra coin in a separate account only for that. Wow! Was I losing it? Why would I begin to stockpile money for jewelry for a girl I had never met? His reply? "You have lived by faith in this romantic world this long; why stop now? If you really believe that she exists and that I will bring her, you will prepare for her before you see her." I stopped in my tracks to chew on that one for a while. The Almighty was right. At this point, all I knew was that God said He was sending her, so by sheer trust in His character, I followed His lead and began to save money for a wedding ring for the wife I'd yet to meet.

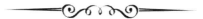

Night shift also meant that I would work Saturday nights when overtime hit. Any socializing that usually happens on the most social of all evenings would be coming to a halt. It also meant that normal sleep patterns would be disturbed, and being up early for church on Sundays would just not happen. There had to be another solution. I recalled this cool church that only met at a local art center on Sunday evenings. Eli, my bass player and best bud, and I visited it a couple of times. This art center had a relatively large room on the upper floor where this church hired a sound company, put up seating, and assembled a church experience where there was none before. The vibe was equally edgy and cool. I dug the band, which included a girl bassist who plucked a McCartney-like Hofner four-string! That was not something you saw every day. The pastor was compelling and very insightful. He was also a riot with his natural humor. I remembered that church well. That could be my answer.

Since my first visit, I learned they had secured a new location in an old funeral home, something more permanent. When 6 p.m. on Sunday rolled around, I was there. And as I suspected, the church had a very artsy vibe where creative humans would feel at home. The band was still good, and I dug the pastor even more. His name was Jeff, and he was a fellow guitarist. After many more Sunday nights, this place would eventually become a new home for me, Eli, and the rest of the band. And to think back now as a married man upon *ALL* I would have missed it if it weren't for that dreaded night shift.

By now, it was early October, and my friend Eli invited me to a couple of Autumn/Halloween parties, both happening on the same Saturday evening. Around 6 p.m., we landed at the first one, which turned out to be a complete bore. Yawn. We found an excuse to bounce out of there early. The second party was on the city's edge, an area I had never been to. The event was outdoors. We had a good time with tasty eats and some cool people to hang with.

The only setback was that the weather was unusually cold for early October. A lot of bodies moved close to the bonfire. It was then that

I first saw her. Have you ever met someone who had instant and overwhelming attraction? Immediately? This was that for me. She sat directly on the other side of the flames in a green lawn chair. This girl had recently arrived as I hadn't seen her before all night. I said nothing but attempted to steal a glance through the fire in her direction whenever I thought it wouldn't be noticeable. It was difficult for me not to stare. This went on for the next hour. Finally, the cold had gotten the best of everyone. You could see our breath in the October night air, and the burning logs in front of us failed to keep us comfortable. Eli and I called it a night. We got up and headed for home.

I hadn't been that stirred seeing a female in a while. It took me back to my teenage years when this occurred for what seemed like every other day. I remember getting away alone and releasing that surprising attraction to Jesus because He was the One who had been working His self-control in me all these years. I knew better than to attempt to handle it in my own ability. Attraction in itself is so fickle and can't be trusted. Peace soon arrived, and I forgot all about the mystery lass by the fire.

Eli and I were hanging out at his house the next afternoon when he dropped a bomb in my lap. "Did you, by chance, see that girl with the dark hair sitting across the fire from us last night?" I nodded while trying not to give away my boyish attraction to her. "Yeah, as it turns out, she was asking about you! Jenny, the girl who hosted the party, called me and told me all about it. She was going to come over and talk to you, but we ended up making tracks before she could. She would like to meet you. Here is her number." Just when I had slain the riot of head noise from the previous night, it started all over again! I dismissed myself once again, stepped outside, and called to Heaven, "You saw what happened to me last night. What's going on with this? Is this Your work? Are You doing something here?" It can be tough not to jump into things out of natural desires when specific opportunities present themselves. I needed perspective, wisdom, and a truckload of self-control.

For many weeks following, we texted each other often. In doing so, I needed to be careful not to allow myself to run away with this in my thoughts. Attraction aside, I honestly wanted to be courteous and converse with her on platonic terms. My free time on the night shift was beneficial; I frequently used that time to intentionally call out to Jesus for His heart on the matter. I needed His constant strength here. She was a big temptation for me. I had close friends pray with me, too. After developing a friendship with her, I knew it was essential to clearly communicate where I stood in the romantic world. Not everyone rolls like I do. I knew I owed her that respect. So, for the first time, I made plans to meet with her. Finally, the night came. We drove to a nearby city to shoot some pool and devour a steaming pizza. I was alert and very sensitive that night; the Spirit of God was present. It was a pleasant and light-hearted time.

From the few hours I spent with her, I could tell we were on different paths. The attraction itself would never be enough to hold something serious together. I knew this was not Heaven's choice of a wife for me. On the way home, I got honest with my new friend, Cecilia. "I am honored that you would be interested in me, but I must tell you that I believe in God-ordained love where He matches people. I have chosen to let Jesus match me, and until He does, I can't be involved in any romantic relationship. I am waiting on Him, hoping and praying that you would too."

She was quiet in response and just nodded in agreement. Honestly, I couldn't tell by her reaction what she thought of what I had just said. That was all good, for I completed the reason for the evening out with her in the first place. Finally, we said our goodbyes with the intention to hang out as friends now and again. Late that night, I received a text from Cecilia. She said the best part of the entire evening was what I had said in the car on the way home. She thanked me. I believe that by the grace given, I was able to deliver what God would have had me say. We never did get together again, and our short friendship quietly dissolved. It was for the best. That's what giving God all your attractions does; it saves hearts from breaking and lives from unfit companions.

Truth be told, waiting with God had brought a very deep satisfaction to my life. If God were never to gift me with a wife I would be ok because I already felt like a rich man in relationship with Him alone.

SCENE TEN

GIRL MEETS BOY

- G -
The Noise We Made

THINKING BACK TO SEVENTEEN YEARS old, standing in a circle, three of us high school dudes with electric guitars slung over our shoulders, and another sitting in the corner behind a set of deep red Ludwigs; I can see something awakened in me that night, and I've never gotten over it. The noise we made in my first band was horrific, as you can imagine, but to my ears, it was angelic. Alongside the amps and drums were lawnmowers, power tools, and lawn furniture. We were in our drummer's parent's garage. Above our heads hung a rather large sign that bore our band name. I was so excited to be in a band that I constructed our very own big old fat rock and roll sign in shop class that proudly announced we existed! Just like the big bands in arenas did. Every week, we were faithful to practice working up new songs, and soon, our little group began to improve. As all budding artists do, we had big plans, but graduation snuck up on us, and the band came to a sudden halt, and we never got out of the garage. The other boys found other priorities. However, I would have done anything to keep it going.

A few months ago, I found our old drummer on social media. I hadn't seen him since graduation day. It was good to hear from him. In our conversation, he told me something I found difficult to believe. He said the band sign I had constructed way back in the day was still hanging in his father's garage. What? Speak of your past coming back to haunt you. I still found it hard to fathom until he sent me a photograph of it. It was nailed to the rafters just as I remembered it, frozen in time! I was seventeen all over again.

Back then, who would have thought that I would still be doing music today? When rock and roll began, it was a young man's game, or so it was initially thought. This genre was brand new, so most people assumed that when we reached a certain age, all these wild kids would outgrow this noise. I never have.

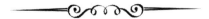

Here I am, no longer a young man, with a new commission from Heaven about to begin a musical endeavor that no one could have seen coming. *Escaping Forevermore* is the tale of Cynthia, a young girl with a divine dream for love the way it should be. Cynthia feels her father's absence, and the evil world agenda of fake love ruled by a hooded ghoul makes plans to ruin her. He presents counterfeits Cynthia falls for until she is on the brink of her heart being ravaged. She is stuck in the lie of fake love from the dark place of Forevermore. Facing the evil world's agenda, it's then that the Savior's redemption reaches her, and He restores the dream of a divine romance she had as a child. Cynthia receives the gift of love and a husband the Savior wanted to give her all along.

While writing *Escaping Forevermore*, thoughts about putting a band together behind the project began. This one was going to take more faith than ever! The band would be called Midnight Valentine. Midnight Valentine represents two things; the first is taken from the book of Ruth when she discovered her God-given husband in the dead of night (midnight). The second is that when Heaven grants a gift of love through another, it could be later in life. I began to share this new vision with various like-minded people around me, all the while asking God for whom He would have to join me. Initially, I thought Midnight Valentine would be what is typically called a "weekend warrior" type of band. That's when you do it for sheer ministry purposes, and you still work a job and play out mostly on weekends and during vacation time. This is a noble approach many Christian musicians adopt because few make it to full-time "rock star" status.

After several false starts with various musicians, three guys eventually emerged with me to form Midnight Valentine. At the same time, I had finished recording the demos of the final versions of songs that would make up *Escaping Forevermore*. We worked those up in sequence to do the live presentation while the film was being edited. As a band, we worked hard and bonded. We began to set some rehearsal times for Bible study and prayer. I planned to combine the influences that inspired me, from being a fan of big-time productions to playing in subculture bands. I used all of these things to mold Midnight Valentine. Some ministry-oriented groups do similar things. These bands fit into church outreach efforts much of the time. I didn't see this as being one of those. I assumed that what we were developing would be a bit "dangerous" and "risky" for some Christians. Although not opposed to playing a church gig, we wanted to create our own event without relying on any venue to supply our needs. So, I invested in our own lighting and sound system. I knew this was God's idea. It was His plan, and we took what we were doing with utmost seriousness.

Images would portray the concept of the story. I wanted something with a high degree of artistic expression, and the perfect image in mind would be a silent film all in black and white. When the time arrived to consider the video portion of *Escaping Forevermore*, I turned to my new church to recruit actors and small support staff.

Still being new to this church, I had begun to meet people. Among them was a blond girl who seemed to be a big deal around these parts. I didn't know what specific role she played in the church. All I did know was that she was some type of leader with pull and authority. Kim was her name. Later, I discovered just how big of a deal she was. First, she was the one who had discovered the building that we were meeting in. Fun fact: I had been in this room (sanctuary) where services were held when it was another church. There were no more than a dozen people there then. And now the place was packed every Sunday evening. The building was formerly a funeral home where dead people hung around. Then I found out that Kim actually named the church. Sheesh! I'd better look out for this one.

Come to find out, Kim was a rocker chick! The girl was not just a fan but had a history of being in tight with rock bands, one band that included the pastor of our church. She naturally took an interest in my musical project to the point that she arranged a "showcase" for us to play after a regular service on Sunday night. I thought this lady had some real clout if she could get the pastor to let us crank some metal after the preaching. The band turned it up. This church metal sound should be a thing every week!

- K -

That Motley Crew

It's early Sunday evening and my birthday weekend. I have a birthday cake "hangover" as I prepare to leave for church. Out of nowhere, I get an impression of what to wear. It was not what I first had in mind, but God spoke to my heart, "I want you to go out with everybody after church tonight." Our church was small enough at the time that everybody congregated at a favorite Mexican restaurant on the north end of town. Best salsa around! I agreed, and it made me understand that what I wore that night mattered to God somehow.

Finances were tight, which is not uncommon for those in a single mom status, but this was a super tight season. I was still a residential supervisor at a transitional care home for that one traumatized young woman trying to get back on her feet. My earnings for this gig were my room and board, and I ate from the local food bank. I worked several odd jobs to supplement that season. Being expected to take part in the customary night out for Mexican was not customary for me. But when you hear God say go, you expect He'll get the check, too.

As the service was letting out that night, my friend Jeff, now Pastor Jeff, asked if I was going out for eats with everyone. To his surprise, I said yes and asked him to save me a seat. Motioning to the back corner of the room, he said, "Cool! We'll be sitting with that motley crew back there."

Our church was a young plant full of young adults and growing fast. Lots of black t-shirts and DYI bleached torn jeans in the seats, including myself, but in knock-off Chuck Taylors. Single moms gotta modify! We started an evening service on purpose. We wanted to set a time apart for our tribe of rock band friends who were most likely hungover on Sunday mornings. The motley crew in the back corner looked like they were friends of our friends. They were "back-in-the-corner of the church" kind of mysterious guys with long hair, tattoos, and musicians. You know the vibe: too cool for school. Of the four, one stood out from the others. He had caught my eye a couple of times in passing as someone familiar. He was statuesque, with a very unassuming energy yet a strong presence. He is one of those creative genius types who is not looking for attention, unbending in his identity. I was looking forward to finally meeting him and his crew.

I was scheduled to close up the building that night, so my arrival at the restaurant was late. The seat left open for me was right next to the creative genius one named Gary. As I sat down, I was introduced to him and his outspoken Nikki-Sixx-looking friend Eli. This Gary dude appeared a bit pestered by my attendance. While everyone was socializing over chips and salsa, he was fixed into conversation with Jeff and not sharing the salsa. With the back of his shoulder toward me, I had to make far reaches with my chips. Occasionally, I'd catch wind of what he shared with my pastor-friend.

I overheard him say something about romantic relationships and writing a book. My head quickly traced back to a dozen conversations I had with a close friend over the years about her friend "Gary," who wrote a book on God's plan for romantic relationships. So many pieces came flying together at lightning speed, and before I knew it, I interrupted him, asking, "Hey, do you know my friend, Megan?"

His head jolted back and said, "Yeah, she's one of my good friends. How do you know her?" I responded the same, "She's one of my good friends, too." I guess he was not impressed because he immediately returned his conversation with Jeff like a man on a mission. Kind of like Nehemiah, who could not be bothered to come down off the wall, this guy, Gary, was a man busy about his Father's business. I was suddenly intrigued to know more about what he was up to and why my church was now his church.

Later that week, Jeff's wife, Stacey, stopped by the beauty counter I was working at. We were catching up on church business, and then she asked what I thought about this new guy. She added, "He's the rocker type you like." Stacey, always a matchmaker, had always kept my romantic interests in mind. Quickly ending her attempts to motivate me, I replied, "I'm intrigued, but showing any romantic interest is in his court, not mine." God said there would be a man who'd hear His voice. I fully expected that the one He spoke of should be the initiator. I had grown into a divine kind of confidence in being fully loved by God. The temptation to reach for attention was gone. He had made me a rich women in relationship with Him. I knew that I knew I was worth the pursuit of His choice and did not have to intice it.

The night I was introduced to him, he gave Jeff his phone number and spelled out a very unusual last name. He said Elliot was his pen name and sounded out his birth name. It was very unusual, but oddly enough, it was also familiar. I decided to do a Facebook search on this guy. I knew I had heard this name before, but where? I attempted a poor spelling of it, and a classmate from my senior year of high school popped up. I'm not sure how she slipped through the cracks, but I never crossed paths with her again once we graduated. I got sidetracked viewing her photos when one came up of her sitting next to this long-haired, sun-burned dude, kicked backed in Chuck Taylors, hat backward, and rock fingers up. It was him. It was Gary! How in the world? Gary was her brother. I had no idea she had a brother. This means this guy could have actually been at my high school graduation. So weird!

My daughter was out of high school by now. I had come to a level of maturity and intimacy in my relationship with Christ that I had no interest in making life happen. I only wanted to respond to His invitations. I knew the value I carried in my relationship with Him. I was beginning to write about it. I knew a book was ahead of me, and I started practicing with a blog. I was getting small opportunities to speak and encourage others to the purpose of eternal life on earth: knowing Him intimately and making Him known.

One of my most memorable events was speaking to a group of women at a new church plant in town. I simply shared from my heart what I was experiencing in my relationship with Christ, finished, and stepped back to my seat, expecting the host to take back the lead in closing the event. When I returned to my seat, everyone appeared stunned, and I realized His Spirit was resting on them heavily. I immediately asked Holy Spirit to help! The hostess took the microphone and said, "Wow, I don't even know how to move forward from this." When all else fails, worship right? And we did. On my way home that night, I was so thrilled at how remarkably Jesus had used me to help these ladies meet Him more deeply. He replied, "You'll see a million faces, and we will rock them all." Yes, Jesus paraphrased a Bon Jovi song lyric. He's just that intimately acquainted with me and all my ways...I cried. I had tasted what was ahead for me. Jesus and I had big ideas of stirring the holiest emotions through my voice to others. There was no way I could begin to guess what man would be best for what Jesus had started in me.

Over the years of trusting God's words to me to remind me of His promise, I vacillated between two typical camps of thought: Is there "the one," or is there one out of many? I had read the top three love stories and saw God's providence presenting one choice to these men. It did not seem out of character to me that God would narrow the road to one. I mean, after all, is that not how He presents His own Son, "the One," to us? Additionally, I did not want to make my own choice. How could I possibly know where life would take us, who would best fit all my weaknesses and best compliment my giftings? I could have never put my life story together as it was being written for my good and the good of others. The thought of choosing for myself, one out of many, left me as the author of my own love story. I had more faith in God's choice than my own because only God can satisfy my longing to see Him glorified as he deserves now and in a future I could never predict. I did not want what I wanted. I wanted what He wanted because He is so deserving of leading every aspect of my life and story. My choice was His choice.

After chatting with Stacey, I was asked to babysit their girls. When I sat in their living room a few days later, Jeff threw a book on my lap called *Who Wants to Fall in Love?* by Gary Elliot. He insinuated, "I started to read it, and all I could think was, 'This sounds like someone I know." Later in the evening, with some skepticism, I opened it up. I got to the third page and stopped. The only way I could explain it was that it felt like I had seen a ghost. All these years walking this romantic road alone, I found a guy like me, one who had been daring in his own faith to wait with God to bring him God's choice. A man who was paying the same price of faith, waiting against all odds for more than he could have imagined for himself. Swirling in my spirit, my intrigue over him turned into prayer: "God, who is this guy, and what are You up to here?"

SCENE ELEVEN

PIZZA & CHERRY DANISHES

- G -
Uncompromising Fire

THE WORLD IS FULL OF pretty people, alluring and attractive. Through the years, with all the "what ifs" I had experienced with the opposite sex, I learned not to be moved by a woman just because she was easy on the eyes. I would not consider a lady based on her appearance alone. Why? I learned that attraction itself is not revelation. There must be more to it than that. I held to that uncompromising fire.

Midnight Valentine was ready to make its premier public appearance. What better place to reveal the band than in the church where we had hoped to find a home? I saw it as a place where we could receive support and be encouraged. On top of that, our church could hold us accountable in order to steward our purpose well. The four of us had rehearsed to the point of running like a well-oiled musical machine. Kim had worked with the pastor to shorten the normal service to open a slot at the end of the evening. We were excited! Ren was known for its high volume and upbeat worship sets. And they did so with excellence. But out and out metal was another monster altogether. This wasn't chiming U2ish anthems, nor was it typical spiritualized Coldplay that was so common for the time. We brought the Mesa Rectifier heaviness! (Ask a metalhead guitarist if you're confused).

I was given the mic for several minutes to introduce the story of *Escaping Forevermore*, the tale of Cynthia, who had a romantic dream but lost her way only to have Jesus restore it. We gave the packed auditorium a sample of two songs. We were very well received. The applause was wonderful and told us that we were doing something right. Even though what we were attempting was outside the ordinary, people understood it. Several humans shared how they sensed God in our efforts. One man, in particular, took me aside and said he could feel the Spirit of God over the room during the first notes of our introduction. "Anointed," he said. Finally, a friendly lady approached me to say how the tale of

Cynthia mirrored her real life. "I lost my way in the arena of relationships, but God redeemed it, just like your story." I thanked her for sharing and asked her name. Her reply? "My name is Cynthia."

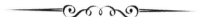

After the "showcase," my new friend Kim continued to take quite an interest in my vision for Midnight Valentine. I got the sense that this was more than just an enjoyable project for her. Something serious was up here. While not fully coming to terms with what was happening at the time, this message and idea seemed to carry a more profound significance for Kim than for the other people involved. Could it be that she is being commissioned to carry this presentation along with us? Well, that was too much information for me to handle then. What I did see in Kim was a passion for the romantic done right and true. She too held an uncompromising fire. Kim was willing to bleed for something she knew to be the truth, which was one of the first things I noticed about her.

Getting to know Kim, I learned she was loyal to her band buddies in days gone by, much more than a fan or support. This girl was what film director Cameron Crow would call a "band-aid," a term from his 2000 film *Almost Famous*. She was in the band's inner circle. Now, Kim showed herself faithful in attending every event Midnight Valentine was involved with. She even arranged and attended our rehearsal at a local church's gymnasium to tweak our sound and lighting systems. I recall her silently praying for us in the back of the room as we worked out the kinks. A mere casual friend with minimal interest would never be involved to the degree she was.

During the production of our silent movie, Kim first took on the role of an administrator to coordinate actors and schedules, something she was excellent at. Then she quit suddenly. Our good friend Sonja stepped in and played a vital role in our project. She sewed custom clothing and constructed rag dolls for props. Sonja was excellent in every way! Kim did return and offered to utilize her makeup expertise to bring our actors to life. The girl always arrived early and worked late. I recall thinking that Kim was the best asset for such a radical effort as *Escaping Forevermore*. I was blessed to have her on board.

- K -
Making Dreams Happen

I really enjoyed being a part of making Jeff and Stacey's "dream" church come true. It was my dream church, too. Before we started, we had aspirations of me being the co-pastor of our new plant. I suggested a name for the church, and it stuck: Renaissance, Ren for short. I was looking forward to developing a volunteer ministry and training people to know and understand their giftedness, all the same things I enjoyed doing at our last church. However, once we got into our first permanent building, a lot of the dreams I had for myself there began to fade.

Walking up from the back parking lot of our new building, I glanced up at the billboard-size sign painted over the back of the old brick building: "Block for Sale." Something in my spirit knew this tiny funeral space we were renting would eventually be a larger space we would eventually own. Currently, Ren owns all three floors of half that city block. That ambitious group of 20 or so who dared to plant this thing had grown to over 1,000 in attendance, and it grew up without me. After about nine months of moving into that old building, God spoke, "I don't want you to drive (lead) anything here."

At first, I was glad to comply until the very next day when I got a text from Jeff, asking me to take the lead in teaching the church. Ugh, God! How do You do that? It's like He knew Jeff was going to be asking this, so He intercepted by giving me the answer to a question I didn't know was coming. I hated saying no to Jeff. It felt like an abandonment of sorts to us both. I had nothing to soothe his disappointment, only God's words to my spirit and a conviction I could not explain. I wanted to finish what I started with them but knew I would not be there in the long run. I knew I was being set apart for something that had not yet been made clear to me.

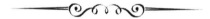

It was around this same time that I began to dare to write. I was starting a book for which I did not know its ending. It was called *Unspent Love*. Years of waiting in faith for the one whom God, my Father, was preparing for me gave me many sympathetic experiences of what it must feel like for Jesus to be waiting for the one His Father was preparing for Him: His Church. I went to a writer's conference in Redding, CA, for some training and directions. All writers give this one piece of advice: No matter what you do, just write, write about something, or write about nothing, but make sure you write. So, I did. I began a blog and published revelations of love and intimacy with Christ and anything else that came to mind during those boring nights at the beauty counter. I didn't know if I was doing it right, but I did it to overcome the perfectionism that commonly paralyzes creatives. Another piece of advice writers give is to get with other writers for critiques and challenges. Gary was the first person I had ever met who had written a book, so I hit him up for a critique of my first couple of chapters. He quickly agreed, and I handed over my first precious few chapters to a guy I just met.

After he had time to read my rough drafts, we met up at one of his frequented pizza dives. I was saturated with curiosity to learn more about his writing process and his purpose with it. Secretly, my curiosity to know what God could be up to between the two of us was growing. Gary was this peculiar balance of towering strength, aloof but thought-filled, laid-back yet hilariously sarcastic. He was a bit of a low-talker, which made me carefully catch all his paced replies to my one million questions. He looked away a lot as though he had to gather his thoughts before commenting. His eye contact seemed to be reserved to bring importance to pivotal points. He was mostly quiet until you asked the right question, and then he'd be an unending source of information and unapologetic opinions, and he ended fun-loving rants with, "I'll educate ya." One thing I appreciated learning about Gary Elliot that first night was that he knew how to hit the ball back into my court and invited me to add in my own "education." It was like he had intentionally learned the value of balanced dialogue and its importance to good relationships. For a dude who had been a bachelor all his days, I was pleasantly surprised at the ease of becoming his new friend.

Eager to get his opinion of my manuscript, which I noticed he had not brought to the table, I asked about it, and he said it was in the car. Inside the car? As I thought that was the whole reason we were meeting at the pizza dive. He added, "Let's go to a coffee joint next and break out the writing." Oh! He had given more thought to this evening than I had. I was expecting a pretty straightforward night, and he threw in an added dimension.

We landed at a coffee joint. Gary paid for the pizza, so I paid for cherry danishes. I enjoyed hanging with him. He was himself without excuses, and the best part was that he was not intimidated by me. I've never considered myself intimidating, but that was the feedback I got a lot until people got to know me as the fun-loving, sarcastic friend I was. I carried myself with a lot of confidence. I was pretty forthright about my convictions and had no problem making decisions. There was also this thing of hearing from God that set me up to be a little intimidating, too. Not that I "read people's" mail, but I knew the path to life in God was a narrow one, and there is a lot of dying to selfish desires, and I was not one to be reserved in telling people you gotta die to live! You know how we have "life coaches" today? Well, I could have been considered a "death coach." Real attractive, right?

Sitting with a man who wasn't intimidated by me or carrying some unworthy complex because they knew my reputation was refreshing. I was new to him. Since I was no one to impress or anyone to fear, he was free to give me exactly what I needed to hear: "Put some cookies in it." He told me my writing was thick, good, and had a heavy impact, but so heavy he said he had to take a break once in a while to recover. He suggested I sweeten it up with some light personal comedy, "You know, put a cookie in it." I went home that night and started to re-read those first chapters and saw precisely what he was talking about. The first heavy point I ran into, I typed: "(insert a "cookie" here)."

I can't say I heard from God that night why our paths were crossing. What I did glean was that this man was intense about following God and sold out to do exactly what God had given him to do. He reminded me again of Nehemiah, a man who refused to come down off the wall of his own "God assignment" to deal with lesser things. Gary was my new friend, a man on a mission, a dreamer who could use some help with his dream.

Our church at that time was dedicated to supporting the arts. We converted our "coffee" gallery to double as an art gallery. Jeff dreamed of our worship team writing their own songs, our members putting on theatrical events, and hosting concerts and comedy improvs. Jeff had agreed to give Gary and his band a few minutes at the end of a service to cast vision for his next movie project, *Escaping Forevermore*, as a launch to recruiting the cast. I love brainstorming through events and projects, so I was an easy pick for Jeff to give the event development to.

Gary and I would occasionally meet over sandwiches and cokes to prepare. I dug, got to know him, and learned what drove his creativity and convictions. Our project meet-ups would always close out with a history lesson from our music experiences in the 80s, movies from the 80s, or what we were doing with our lives in the 80s. At the end of one of our project meetings, he mentioned an earlier film he attempted. The filming had been completed, edited, and then lost. All the digital art crashed. He described it as more of a fairytale where his actors wore forest animal costumes. His creative imagination was so intriguing. I asked him, "What was it called?" He replied, "When Violet Dreams." What!?! I think I quietly choked on my Jimmy John sub when he said, "Violet." What in the world was going on here? Somehow, I was able to move past my interior shock and pressed, "Violet? Why Violet?" Waiting for some deep, profound revelation that God had given him concerning violets and promise and a wife, and expecting the Heavens about to split open with a choir of angels to declare the revolutionary will of God, he replied, "I don't know. I just dig the name."

SCENE TWELVE:

FACETS OF VIOLET

- G -
Enchanting

VIOLET. WHAT AN ENCHANTING NAME.

I remember the evening well. An older lifelong friend who loves all things theatrical was in the Nissan with me. Our destination? I-55 South for St. Louis, Missouri. We had tickets for Edward Scissorhands, the touring play based on the Tim Burton classic film. I happened to be in the arched city a couple of months back and spotted a poster in a window advertising the upcoming presentation. For me, this was a play not to be missed. I had loved the movie for decades and found it a pleasant surprise that someone would produce a musical of such a strange story. We were both thrilled!

On the trip down, my buddy and I were extra chatty. I guess our excitement was showing.

As of late, I have found myself in a season of waiting for what was next. Much of what I had been involved in reached their conclusions, and now it was time for something new. This period felt like the calm before the storm, but I didn't yet know what the storm was. After much prayer, I had been listening closely to Heaven, expecting revelation for some time now. Little did I know, it was about to arrive, and it would be what I never could have predicted.

During my conversation with my elderly friend, Jesus was going to give me an assignment. I'm not even sure what my buddy said, but his words triggered the Spirit of God to communicate to me, "Make a movie." That was it; that was what's next. I have always been a movie buff and an armchair critic at that. I had taken in enough films to have a clue between what is a treasure and what is rubbish. At least in my own mind. But to actually attempt to make my own movie? Man, that's another thing altogether. But before I had any time to object or argue with God, I knew what the film was to be about. Also, I knew who to call.

I sat through the entire play with my head abuzz. I'm going to make my own movie. I believed it. The next afternoon, I grabbed my phone and whispered a prayer, "If this is what you have for me, you must put this together." The proposal was made to my friend, who, by the way, had experience in filmmaking; he was on board. Plans were being made on the spot. At once, things began to move at a frantic pace. In slightly more than three weeks, we would begin shooting. In less than a month, I went from a divine "whisper" to "action." A cast was assembled, locations secured, and sets were designed. Remember the calm before the storm? Well, I quickly found out what the storm was. I purchased costumes, painted props, and ran my tail off. Most of my day was occupied with getting this movie off the ground.

Oh, did I forget to mention that we needed a screenplay? Yeah, we had to have one of those. I had basic outlines for the story already developed, but those would need to be fleshed out. They needed much work. When I had free time at my employment, I wrote. During my commute home, I scribbled (safely). And on nights and on the weekends, you could find me in front of a glowing screen and keyboard. The deadline was approaching, and the first day of shooting was just around the corner. At last, the story was ready. I was now at the place to begin the final draft. Planting myself behind the computer once again, I typed, *When Violet Dreams.* Why Violet? It's always been a bit of a mystery to me. I never labored over what to call the main character. Somehow, I just knew her name was to be Violet. Enchanting!

- K -

Violets in the Snow

Are you old enough to remember the national television broadcasting system signing off at midnight? The screens would blink a color bar code and then go to snow; black and white static visually and audibly. That was me when Gary said, "When Violet Dreams." My brain turned into a 1970 TV static snow.

In my promise, violets had filled every yard surrounding every home my daughter and I lived at by this time, starting with our first home, apartment number seven, for seven years. There had been a particularly lingering winter in central Illinois as well as in my soul. I had been believing God's promise of a man who would hear His voice just as He said for seven years, and I was growing weary. Spring was trying to stake its claim, but winter was relentless. One morning, on my way to work and feeling the winter blues a little more deeply than usual, I opened the door to a fresh dusting of snow. Only this time, my familiar sleeping bed of violets was springing to life anyway. Yes, I saw "Violets in the Snow." My doubting heart thawed at remembering His gift to me as I saw promise pushing up through the adversity of an unseasonal winter blanket.

That seventh year was the end of an ordinary Christian life for me. Acts of faith were about to take the lead. Daring prayers, unusual circumstances, and following God's voice into mysterious leadings would color the next decade of my single mom experience, and the seasonal wild violets would remain, filling the landscape of my faith in God's words to me. Never did I imagine that on the other side of town, this whole time, there would be a man writing songs and divine romantic films about a girl named, of all things, Violet.

We had a great time setting up Gary's recruitment launch for Escaping Forevermore. I don't believe that old funeral space had ever heard the noisy sounds of an art metal band before. The people who attended were impressed, not just with the music but also with Gary's heart. It was pure and felt by everyone who came, and the volunteers began to line up. After touching base with Gary, he was really touched by everyone's response and somewhat surprised. The years of walking the narrow road of believing God for a wife and a national ministry to encourage the masses in God's ways in the romantic were peeking out from behind his excitement. I, too, was touched to have had a part in helping his dream catch some air that night.

Over the next couple of weeks, I worked with Gary, lining up the volunteers and helping him identify the individuals I thought would best fit the characters in his film. The project began to build momentum. I found myself looking forward to seeing Gary and then disappointed our exchanges were only "business" in nature. I would get home feeling deeply dissatisfied that I wasn't experiencing more in my relationship with him. My frustration was not making any sense. There was no misleading going on. Then, it dawned on me; my curiosity about him was turning into an attraction for him.

I had yet to hear from God His intentions for this new friendship, so I did what I had learned over the years to be in the best interest of my newly troubled heart. I gave these affections to God and became intentional about the time and space I would share with Gary. I quit the administrative responsibilities he needed for the film. Thankfully, one person in particular was not interested in acting but was passionate about doing anything else to help the project. Sonja was a high school classmate. She had recently returned to central Illinois after enduring a painful divorce. She was eager to help and highly administrative. I explained the trouble my heart was experiencing and confided to her that I was curious if God might not be lining Gary and me up. At this point in my faith, I knew that attraction is not God's voice, and when attraction comes, it is best to distance myself from it until God's thoughts regarding a relationship are clear to me. Take note: Feelings come from thoughts. Change your thoughts to God's thoughts, and your feelings will follow.

Over the next few months, I would check in on him, visit a couple of gigs the band was playing, and take my new distancing as an opportunity to observe him prayerfully. I saw a lot of intensity from him when it came to dreams and character. I saw a lot of playfulness when it came to hanging with others. We occasionally texted, through which I learned he still owned a dumb phone. It was 2013, and this never-married single guy did not allow himself to be alone with internet access at home or on his phone. His conviction took my breath away. Completely ungoverned in his own house, he refused the temptation of culture's over-sexualization and porn. What? I've heard of guys finding accountability partners, adding software to their computer system to tattle on them when they crossed the line, but refusing the easy access altogether. Wow!

I could not believe a man who lived alone, free to peek with no one around, was walking the planet, choosing to live without the convenience of auto-fill texting, hand-held emailing, and instant social media access. Gary Elliot was not only a man who was determined to receive God's gift in a wife but also determined to live out his life as a pleasure to God *and* his future wife. He was a man full of faith and the Holy Spirit's power to live a life worthy of his calling.

Something in me shifted at the knowledge of this peculiar discipline in Gary's life. He was a man of God, not in the way of a title or a sentimental reminder of biblical identity. No, he was a man of God as in dedication, love, and honor to Him. I had not encountered this stature of male Christianity in the ordinary church culture. I only encountered this stature in senior church leaders, men, and women who had a lot on the line regarding influence and responsibility. A deep respect rooted in me for him, as though something holy was at work between him and God. There was a new conviction in me that I would not dare to distract him from God's plans and purposes for him, including whom God would choose to be this man's wife. Curious circumstances and flashes of attraction don't make it God's choice. God's voice makes it God's choice, and that's all I ever wanted. Too many times, we take the lead, follow the desires of our hearts, and ask God to bless it. But He is the One Who paid the highest price for our lives. Therefore, we should desire to follow in love by letting Him take the lead concerning our desires and give Him the liberty to challenge and change them where needed. God said there would be a man who hears His voice. The responsibility to make us known to one another as more than friends rested on God, not us, and that's the same place I left my affections—on God. I practiced a lot of gratitude for His faithfulness over the years to walk me into His tangible reminders of violets, flashes "33", and remembrances of the many words He had spoken to keep in His faithfulness. These encounters were like food to my spirit.

I remember taking a road trip with one of my sweet young friends who was waiting with God for her promised husband, too. We created a kind of retreat weekend of sorts. We headed out of state to a ministry campus where we both gleaned so much intimacy with Christ from over the years. Together, we sat in a room for ministry intercessors to pray over us and relay anything that was on God's mind for us to know. The young man sitting across from me said in his mind's eye (spirit) he saw a very large clock like a pocket watch, hanging over me. He was getting an impression from God to encourage me to know, "It's time. However, it is time but not like it's time on a clock but more like a season of time, and now that it's time it's about timing."

I took that to understand it really is time for my promised marriage and within this time its reality will come about in His timing. I tucked this experience in my heart to quietly ponder until God said more. And boy, did He soon say more.

SCENE THIRTEEN

GOD PROPOSES

- K -

Decades of Unspent Love

THERE WAS AN ORDINARY DAY within this mysterious friendship with Gary when I went to lunch and landed in the parking lot of a nearby lake to talk to God. "God, what's going on here? I see so many parallels." He responded with three pieces of wisdom: "Let him take the lead. Let him define the relationship. Don't look at him as though there was something wrong with him, and don't look back for something to be wrong with yourself." That was it. That's all He said. It was a leading of sorts, but to what?

So, let's catch up here: This is a man of daring faith. He is a man with a mission, a rock musician with long hair, an author, a man waiting (a long time, I might add) for God to present his wife, and a man who wrote a movie script called *When Violet Dreams*. Don't tell me you wouldn't be more than curious at this point. You may be hopeful this is the "one," right? Of course, you would be, and I was. But he's not mine. I only had hope based on glowing coincidences and a handful of wisdom nuggets from God on stewarding this new friendship, but no word confirming this was His choice for me.

Freeing myself from imagined expectations, God had not only built my confidence in His pure desire and perfect ability to set me up with the one He wanted for me, but I was actually excited to let those expectations go and stay in a place of being surprised, wanted, and pursued. I had had a deep season in the waiting where my worth before God exceeded my imagination. I knew God, and I was quite the catch because He lived in me. I remained friendly with Gary according to the wisdom God gave me and kept up on the film project with Sonja. After some time, I sensed a peace that I could go ahead and offer my skills as a make-up artist as needed.

Then something crazy happened.

I got a life-threatening interruption. I suffered a pulmonary embolism within three weeks of starting a new job. I was near death, according to the charts. They had me in the Cardiac ICU for seven days, and I was bored out of my mind. Jeff came to see me. He and Stacey had seen me overcome many challenging circumstances over the years. He took a seat in the corner of my hospital room. Jeff casually asks, "So, whatcha thinking?" I reply, "I'm thinking I need to call for the church's elders, but *I am* the elder of our church." We both laughed. Planting a church full of young people had us both in need of some seasoned church-elder kind of wisdom and prayers.

I came out of that experience with three rewards: a new felt presence of Jesus the whole time that reminded me of my mother's cheek pressing on mine when I was sick as a little girl. Though He never said a word, He was tangibly with me like no other time in my life. Second, I came out with a $75K hospital bill because I was between insurance plans. However, the hospital favored my appeal and waived it. It felt like a miracle! Lastly and most impacting was my daughter's response. She stayed at home, alone for days, without her mom for the first time, even though she had offers from family friends to stay with. I asked her if she was ever afraid of losing me. She replied, "No, I know you have a call on your life, and no way was God done with you yet." Her faith in Him was my greatest reward in that experience.

It is bewildering to look back now and see how close I was to coming into a lifelong promise being fulfilled when death attempted to step in first. I don't know how exactly the spiritual realm works regarding our bodies, but you can be sure I was paying attention. I was more resolved than ever that our lives are in God's hands. Sometimes, He allows by His great wisdom what He can easily stop by His great power. Our job is to stay in faith that God is good all the time. He stands inside the solution we need, and He has already made a plan to fit all things into the primary plan of transforming us more and more into the image of His beautiful and powerful Son.

It was not an emotionally devastating experience, as though my heart needed a year to recover. It was more like a blip on the screen of my life. That Monday, I was right back to work, finished my new job training, and relocated to my permanent office location. Sonja had reached out to schedule me for some make-up needs for a big shoot at a park across the town. The band had just bought a touring RV, and I would get to use it as my make-up studio. It sounded like fun, even if it was a DIY-grade kind of fun. The summer heat was begging to turn itself up while filming was progressing. It was so much fun to be a part of something that creative in our dry little city. Gary's talent and imagination were impressive and daring. He was a bit of a perfectionist, which included his direction in my make-up skills. Occasionally, he'd take a character or two and enhance my efforts. I was the elegant make-up artist getting lessons on gothic under-eye dark circles, which are so much more dramatic than your evening smokey eye look. Overall, it was fun, light, and freeing. It did my heart good to help, come and go as I pleased, and make some friends—no more disappointed imaginations.

August 1, 2013, to be exact. I was sitting at my new desk. Our lobby was quiet, with very little customer traffic. Out of nowhere, I felt an intense weight of God's presence upon me. I just started to praise and talk to Him in my heart until I could no longer focus on the tasks at hand. I knew I needed to get away to a quiet place and settle on what God was trying to bring my attention to. I excused myself to the ladies' restroom. It was the only place in the building where I could have any privacy. I stood there for a minute, asking God what He wanted and what I could do for Him. Within my heart, He asked me a question, "Would you take him as your husband?" I knew immediately that "him" was Gary Elliot. Feeling caught off guard, I replied with my first thought, "No."

I quickly rehearsed in my mind what I saw in my relationship with him: "I don't see that he desires me or has been given the capacity to honor me as a wife." God replied, "But, would you take him for what you *do* see?" What *do* I see? I began to review all the attributes I had come to see in this man. His high integrity, his passion for his dream, his devotion to knowing God and making God's desires in the romantic known, as well as his pure heart. He, too, had been hidden in Christ as I had been. Then my thoughts rolled unto his wait; he is a bridegroom with decades of *unspent love,* decades of unspent love like me. That was the name of the book I was writing at the time: *Unspent Love.* At that point, I lost it. Our parallel lines crossed in my spirit, and I began to weep over the undeniable caliber of a man who had been set apart for the wife God would choose for him. I could not say no. I said, "Yes, how could I not."

There are moments within the normal Christian life when God says one thing, and it overturns everything you once desired and everything you once feared. You are changed in a moment. From that day forward, you remember the date, the place, and the pivot that took place in your life. That word becomes an anchor in your spirit to keep you in it, come what may. It's not that I became fully convinced, but I did become fully committed to seeing it through to God's satisfaction. Faith comes by hearing Him, and the manifestation of what is heard is an uphill climb. Even though you now know the end of a thing from its beginning, you still have to play the game in between. There will be good plays, bad plays, fouls, injuries, and points gained. It will be thrilling and transforming, and God will get what He wants from it whether we fully understand it at the time. He is not looking for us to understand His words. He is looking for us to say yes without understanding. This is the faith that pleases Him and changes us.

Because faith is a growing thing, I lasted seven days before I questioned what God had said. While sitting in line at a McDonald's drive-thru, I asked, "God, are you sure you have us in mind for one another?" I glance up from the question in my heart to a billboard staring me in the face, titled "The Perfect Match," featuring a professional husband and wife team. That was the beginning of many more passing doubts to be refuted by perfectly timed glances.

You know that time John said, "Jesus did many other things as well. If every one of them were written down, I suppose that even the whole world would not have room for the books that would be written"?

This is that part of our story. This book does not have room for everything God did to keep me in the faith that a single encounter provided. It had been 21 years since God first spoke to my mother, "There will be a man who hears My voice." Twenty-one years of growing in grace, growing in love, and growing in faith. Twenty-one years laced with longing, hoping, and wondering "if" and "when." Twenty-one years of coming out of self-hatred, self-pity, and self-centeredness. Twenty-one years of coming into my true identity, understanding my purpose and my giftedness.

Twenty-one years of my life had been preserved within a nested life of deepening companionship with the only Lover of my soul, Jesus. I fell in love with the One who loved me first before it was time for Him to share me. I recall, shortly after my daughter and I moved into our first apartment, when God spoke to my heart, "You know how to be in a loveless relationship." It startled me. I desperately wanted to be in love, married, and complete my family with a man of God. In the middle of what I thought was a pure desire for love, God interrupted that perception with a truth I had never known about myself before that moment. I was the daughter of a father who did not know how to love me well growing up, and it resulted in me having low expectations of a man's love and the marital experience. I had a choice in that moment to follow my own withered desires or His voice regarding those desires. For the sake of myself and my daughter, I could not repeat another love-less relationship. He says in His word that He will give you the desires of your heart, so I surrendered my desires for love to His desires. I surrendered to His deconstruction, healing, and transformation. He became my ultimate satisfaction, security, and confidence. He enabled me to slow down and allow wisdom to teach me what was best for me instead of what the culture was preaching to me. Everything I had learned from being a companion of Jesus prepared me to follow Him further into the fulfillment of His promise to me and to love a man only He would reveal.

How does a girl who believes she has heard from God who her husband is move forward in that? Um, carefully and prayerfully. God said to let Him take the lead and define the relationship, so there was nothing for me to do but say yes to Gary as I said yes to God. I brought my new insights to a couple of close friends, including Jeff, who was my pastor. I never thought walking alone was wise when God reveals life-changing opportunities. To walk in the counsel of many is biblical and wise. All of them kept watch with me but one. She was new to understanding what waiting with God was like and took my new understanding straight to Gary. The next thing I knew, Gary invited me out for pizza to "talk."

I wish I could tell you God was setting Gary up to know what I was knowing, and this pizza date would be the beginning of a sweet romance, but I can't. I was really nervous. I knew that I knew I was about to be friend-zoned. How would I respond? What's God going to do about what He started in me? Gary and I met for pizza and started discussing how the movie project was coming along. After the tension was too much, Gary finally addressed why he asked me to meet with him. He told me he had heard from a friend that I was expecting more than a friendship with him. He was very sober, adding, "This is as far as this goes." He explained how much he appreciated my friendship and said I was a blast to hang out with. He said he wanted to be friends, and it would make him very sad not to be my friend any longer. The whole time he was zoning me, I had total peace. I was not wounded nor disappointed. In fact, deep inside my spirit, I sensed God was giggling. Yeah, giggling. It was as if He knew this was not the end of His words to me concerning Gary but just the beginning. It was weird, but it was real. Gary defined the relationship as friends only, and I as God prepared me to do, I honored it.

Within a week, Gary texted me an invitation to a Stryper concert. It had been years since I had been to a rock concert. Since I started following Jesus, I no longer had any friends who shared my love for live rock. Now I had one. I believe God had planned for us to marry. Gary believes I am only destined to be his friend. I want to keep my distance, and I want to go to a rock show. I'm straight-up conflicted and start talking to God about what to do. Mid-sentence, I get a text from a friend. He said he was praying for me, and in the middle of his prayer, he saw an image, in his mind's eye, of a giant hand holding out a rose like on the tv show The Bachelor. The hand was extending this rose to me as an offering to come with Him. I knew immediately that was God's answer to me. That was God extending the invitation to come further into friendship with Gary. I had the assurance to say yes to the rock show and that God was moving me past the recent objections and further into the mystery of His unfolding words to me.

Our friendship grew from the many things we were passionate about, like 80s rock being the best decade of music ever, tattoos, rock-a-billy subculture, movies, people watching, abstract creativity, God-given purpose, and the values of waiting with God. He introduced me to baseball, the Chicago Cubs specifically, arcades, and haunted houses. It took him three years of inviting me with his friends to his annual Halloween joy of haunt-hopping to wear me down to one yes. I only went so that he would stop asking me. The only thing I like about a haunted house now that we are married is holding his hand as he laughs at the props and high-fives the monsters for successfully startling him.

Our times together as friends consisted of a couple of texts in a week, catching up at church, and hitting a show or an event of some sort every other month or so. Helping out with his film project was a random activity. Getting everybody in the same place at the same time was difficult and would put filming off for weeks. It was also broken up a lot by trips Gary had to make to South Carolina, where his dad was fighting cancer. His family had relocated there early on, and was a second home to him. In these times, our conversations took deep dives into purpose, future hopes, and support with difficult decisions.

One of the topics of interest we shared more closely than all others was waiting with God for the one God would have for us to marry. Whenever the conversation came around to it, our passions would simultaneously flare. Our love for God's desires over our own was strong. We both hoped for impossible things God had spoken to us over the years, and still believing without seeing reinforced the parallel races we were running. So much so that in those times, I thought I could be wrong about what God asked of me, and I'd consider a compromise; maybe we just run together but with different spouses. Then God would throw me a reminder of His pure desire: another billboard displaying that exact "Perfect Match" advertisement or Gary throwing a book in my lap on the marriage covenant with a cover image of parallel ribbons crossing over each other, more sprinkles of "33", or another violet "sighting" but now coming up in conversations with Gary and not just my yard. Throughout our entire friendship, God never left me alone in my thoughts of this being anything less than what He had said.

It took a lot of discernment to help me stay within the boundaries God gave me. Sometimes, I wanted to do more to encourage him, and God would say no. Then, there were other times when God would direct me to encourage him, and I'd want to say no. I followed through, of course, but it made for waves of affection I would have to ride and simultaneously taste the many fruits of self-control. There were many tugs of war between what I felt and heard. There were many temptations to quit waiting or manipulate a circumstance in my favor. I was learning the importance of anchoring to His words when your number one desire is God's pleasure over you. I remember completely minding my own business one Saturday afternoon, sitting at the dining room table assorting bills, and God spoke to my spirit, "It's good for you to wait with Me while you wait for him." And it was. It was making me strong in my spirit, growing me in the experiences of the knowledge and wisdom of God, and building unshakeable levels of faith. In the end, and best of all, it proved all the accusing voices wrong; I was never crazy to believe what God said; I was never crazy to follow Him; I was actually faithful.

After a little over a year, our passion for this message of God's desired role in our romantic lives crossed, and it ignited a mutual desire to lead a small group together to encourage others in this faith. Get this: Our first small group meeting was on Valentine's Day. It was the first time Gary and I partnered equally on a ministry effort. He was the profound precept guy, and I was the relational insight girl. He would bring things to the table I had not considered before and match them to insights I had gained through my own experience and understanding. It was hard not to show my excitement over how well-fitted we were for this message.

On one of the more memorable evenings, Gary revealed to the group how God had asked him to save up his overtime money for the wedding ring he would give his wife. My insides melted at the thought! He was called to exercise his faith by saving up for the wife he had not met yet. While looking for a new church where unknown to him, his future wife actually was—ARE YOU KIDDING ME? That was another opportunity for me to see that while God was preparing me for Gary, He was also preparing Gary for me.

The weekend that followed this announcement, my father stopped by to bring me what remained of my mother's jewelry. He said it was mine to do with what I will. I was surprised that her original 1964 wedding ring was included in his giveaway. So many memories of her warmth, elegance, and strength came over me to see it again. I took the gems to the jeweler for an appraisal. It was more generous than expected, and I decided to cash in. However, there was something about the wedding set I could not let go of. It was not a set I had ever imagined wearing myself someday, and it was way too small for me. And the original center diamond was missing. All I did know was that I could not yet part with it. I stored it in the attic until further notice, along with the irony of Gary's recent savings instruction.

The remainder of the year was full of narrowing my vision for where God wanted my voice. He asked me not to move away from this message of the romantic and to expect to see the moral compass of a generation turn toward waiting with God for His answers to their longings out of a desire to know Him rather than out of a transactional duty to appease Him. The more we move past the idea of God being a religious taskmaster and into His true nature as a Good Father, our hearts turn over within us to desire to make His dreams come true like Jesus did and waiting will no longer feel like something we have to do but something we want to do. My book, Veiled Unto His Pleasure, opens with the Hebrew definition of waiting, which is to intertwine with the One you are waiting with, not waiting for, but waiting *with*. Time spent intertwining with the One Who brought His life and promises results in a love relationship that settles you once and for all.

A lot of what intertwining looks like is praying and communing with God as He is fashioning both sides of the promise. My time was filled with intercession for Gary and his band. At one point, I shared with him that while in prayer with God, I saw my wedding dress, the train filled with gold serving utensils, saying there will be an outpouring of this message once you cross the threshold of your wedding. It stirred in him the remembrance of a word someone gave him of jewels spilling from his heart as he declared his own story. See, both sides are being fashioned at the same time when you're waiting *with* God.

By the next Valentine's Day, he and I were driving home from a full day of ink, pizza, and a Valentine-themed haunted house event we enjoyed with one of our friends in Chicago. I had gotten my first violet tattoo. It was the first time I shared with Gary its significance. In turn, he told me he had just written a new song called "When Violet Dreams." I'm screaming on the inside, "Our parallels are not ironies! There is no question that they are divine!" It was a fight to not join in on the accusations that there was something wrong with Gary for not seeing what I was seeing. His love for God and His will was as strong as his character. God's Spirit, the same Spirit in me, the same Spirit in Jesus, dwelt in Gary, too. He did not see me as more than a friend because God had not lifted the veil for him to see me yet. I had to deal with my attitude of being a friend of God. You know, as a prophetic person, God does nothing until He first shares it with His prophets. I am supposed to consider it a privilege to keep God's secrets like a friend, but I had my days where I was definitely not feeling the honor of it.

Occasionally, I would visit a church in Champaign for a change of sound and scenery. They had a significant guest speaker one night. One I was particularly endeared to. He recalled a time when God gave him a new friend. A friend whose personality grated him in all the wrong directions. He told God he thought this friendship was a bad idea; there was just something wrong with this guy, or maybe something wrong with himself. God replied, "I think you are perfect for each other. There is nothing wrong with him. There is nothing wrong with you (because you are both complete in Christ). There is only something missing." He explained that what was missing was light, a revelation of the next thing God wanted to bring into the relationship. Oh, the freedom! The exact words God spoke to him were a gift of more understanding to me. There is nothing *wrong* with either of us. There is only something missing; the next revelation is missing, and we know who is the Light of revelation, the One of perfect timing.

On Mother's Day, 2015, Gary texted a pic of a flier announcing an Ink and Iron Festival in Nashville coming in August. This was an inaugural event out of the annual Santa Barbara event. We are talking tattoos, rock-a-billy, and live rock shows. I was in immediately, with or without Gary. Within a month of his invitation, I am in prayer for one of Gary's band members when God says to my spirit, "Nashville Matters." It sounded familiar, but I could not recall its first mention. I pulled out my computer and hit the "find" button. There it was, journaled in 2008, "Nashville Matters." Gary's band was hitting a lot of walls with opportunities and bandmates; considering he, I, and his vocalist were attending the festival together, I shared it with them to be aware that our visit may have more in store than just a fun time.

The three of us agreed to be prayerful about Nashville mattering in the weeks leading up to our road trip. On June 13, 2015, I was sitting on my couch, spending time with God in His Word and prayer. I was conflicted. I thought Nashville mattered in 2008 when He first spoke about it, and nothing came of it. I could see how Music City would matter for the band but not for me. I asked Him, "Why me, why now?" He replied very clearly, "Because Tennessee is where your virtue was raped from you, there is now, therefore, an inheritance there for you."

I can't explain the breaking that took place in me at His words. It was as though a reward awaited me that I had not been expecting. Choosing life was the right thing to do. Being Andee's mom was and still is rewarding all by itself. To think there was more to come was overwhelming. More to be enjoyed in the land of violation is astounding, as though God Himself had plans to enjoy great revenge on His enemies in that state. These are weak descriptions of what I felt, but it was so intense that I began to sob. I tried to be quiet because Andee was in her room, still asleep. I failed. She came out of her room to see why I was crying. I told her God just spoke to me. She responded, "Oh, then everything is okay." I replied, "Yes, they are happy tears." I went on to tell her what He said. For the first time in our relationship, she responded with a very assured peace that if I were to move, it would be good, and she would be okay.

The next person I told, of course, was Gary.

SCENE FOURTEEN

GOD HAS HIS SECRETS

- G -

Ink and Iron

IDNIGHT VALENTINE REHEARSED DILIGENTLY on Friday evenings. On one particular Friday, we decided to set some time apart for praying and asking God what His plans were for this musical endeavor. I didn't want to assume something myself and project those assumptions on God, but I wanted to hear His heart from the beginning. I had mentioned earlier "weekend warrior" bands that still held day jobs and performed mainly on weekends. These groups weren't concerned with making music a full-time career. This was my experience with bands, and I assumed that's what Midnight Valentine was destined for. But on this night, that perception of the band changed from what I thought it first to be. After asking God about His plans, we sat in silence for a short while, waiting for Heaven's answer. I had a powerful sense that the weekend paradigm wasn't what He had in mind after all. I believed that God wanted to take this work to a national level. This is where the faith gets thick. I love music as much as ever but have no desire to strive and scratch to "make it" in the music world. All I want is to finish what the Lord calls me to do, and whatever that looks like is up to Him. I'll strap on my Charvel Super Strat for merely a dozen people, give it all I've got, and be content. But Jesus has said He wants more than I imagined for this, and even now, though I've grown older, I still believe His words.

I was at a place of convergence when Kim was getting divine downloads on Nashville. All the efforts to move Midnight Valentine forward in the Midwest had been falling short for some time now. Midnight Valentine only played a handful of live shows when we began to sense doors were closing in our home state of Illinois. Through various happenings, I, too, began to get a clue that God was saying to take this music to Nashville. Without question, it would be a massive undertaking. Lots of prayers went into the decision. Over time, I became convinced that it was the right thing for the project and that Music City would be the place where its redemptive message would eventually rise to a national platform.

During this same time, I learned that my 26-plus-year gig at the auto factory was coming to a close. The entire department walked the long and deserted hallway to an exit next to the offices near the north end. This once busy and sprawling auto plant was closing its doors forever. After working with everyone for that long, today would be the last time I would see most of these people. In just a few minutes, we would sign the last of our release papers and turn in our access badges. That "short time" of working at the auto plant that I had hoped for was finally ending after more than two and a half decades. That's far from a short time. Many people were sad. I saw more than a few tears. I, on the other hand, was a little melancholy but mostly happy because of what God told me years back about my desire for a wife of His choice. I knew long-awaited promises of love and purpose lay ahead. Never did I expect to remain here that long. I learned that the ways of the Divine and human logic don't work very well together.

I knew for sure that middle Tennessee was where I was headed. I began to pack stuff up at my house, ready for the move. But after much consideration, the rest of the band would not be going the distance with me. The first and original version of Midnight Valentine would eventually be no more. I knew now that we were together for a season, not for the duration. The announcement that the auto factory was calling it a day for manufacturing in the States immediately made me know that this was my open door to Tennessee.

I have always favored retro 50s and 60s vibes. Old classic cars have always been a weakness for me. I especially dig the mid-50s Chevys, some of the most sought-after collectibles ever. One thing I've learned about myself is that I must keep a lid of self-control over my love for these old beauties, or it may bite me in the bum. Oh yeah, it's happened before. Here is a painful example.

A harsh mistake was made long ago when I took off to run an errand one Saturday afternoon and returned with an emptied-out bank account and a black and white '57 Chevy. It needed quite a bit of care. This was nothing more than a compulsive purchase. I found her in the driveway of a neighborhood house I had never been to. There was a red for sale sign hanging boldly in the rear window. The thought was that it couldn't hurt to stop and look. Yeah, be careful with that one! And in that look, there were three issues that I never bothered to consider before writing a fat check that day. First, I had very little knowledge of car restoration. Second, I had no access to a facility for such an endeavor. Third, purchasing the car itself left me with empty pockets and hardly any resources left to take on a classic overhaul.

My new purchase would require repainting, re-chroming, an interior makeover, engine rebuilding, and transmission replacement. Dude, I was massively in over my head. Eventually, I rebuilt the motor and got a sloppy paint job, but she was still without a transmission. The relic sat stalled at my parents' house for a couple of years. In time, I sold it for a significant loss. The moral of this tale is that I still dig these old machines from yesteryear as much as ever, but if I ever owned another, it must already be restored. (It wouldn't hurt if I had deep pockets, either.)

Scanning through the magazines at a megastore, I found one advertising a retro-styled festival coming to middle Tennessee in late summer. The Ink and Iron Festival originated in California and has expanded to Nashville. This full-page color ad intrigued me. I had been to many festivals through the years, all kinds of full-blown metal and hard rock fests, goth events, radical Christian festivals, mainstream Christian fests, and more. I had been a part of various bands that also played some of these events. The Ink and Iron Festival was different, unlike any I'd attended. It was a mixture of tattoo culture, an eclectic mixture of song artists, vintage bikes, and hot rods, including, of course, '57 Chevys. Much of it was rockabilly. What I found so fun was that this fest would have some of the original artists who helped birth the entire genre back in the 50s. A slew of current rockabilly artists was on the slate, as well as modern metal, horror punk, and a couple of outlaw country legends. Eclectic enough? Man, I wanted to go to this. At once, I took a photograph of the ad and sent it to Kim, knowing she would also dig it. So, within a few days, three of us friends scheduled time off, secured lodging at a local hotel, and had our tickets in hand. Exciting!

By August, the three of us found ourselves in Bicentennial Park in the middle of Nashville for Ink and Iron fun. The tattoo madness took place up the hill a few blocks at the Municipal Auditorium, a

Nashville original. Upon first entering the domed circular arena, I'd never heard such unison of buzzing ink machines. Hundreds upon hundreds of tattoo artists from all over the lower 48 were going at it at once. It was quite a scene and a great experience. We all got inked!

Rockabilly music is a blast. It's where country swing and fiery blues, where rock and roll began its hot notes. There were times that I wished I had grown up during its inception. That era always held a deep appeal to me. We had made it a point to see as many rockabilly bands as possible throughout those few days. It had us hopping all over the park to various stages.

Although the collection of classic rides was not large in size, there were some unique and exquisite projects to behold. Once again, I felt the itch and urge to possess a beauty for myself. In my mind, I began to plot and scheme how to move certain monies around in order to purchase such a ride as several of them were displaying for sale. Then, in a sudden surge of sanity, I recalled my younger days of compulsive purchases, including a particular '57 Chevrolet that had my lunch for a long time! It was time to get away from all the relic rides and find another band to listen to.

With all the fun and frolic we were surrounded with, more important issues were at hand. With the fast approaching end of my job just around the corner, I knew this beautiful southern city was to become my new home. Throughout these three days, I asked God how He wanted me to get here. I needed some direction, a word from Heaven. I wasn't alone. All three of us were looking forward to relocating to Music City. None of us had a clue how this was going to happen. Ink and Iron concluded, and I had received no revelation from the Heavens.

Before leaving town, Kim had arranged a lunch with a friend she knew who lived in Nashville. Her friend's father was a pastor of a church they had started in the area decades earlier; they were originally from Los Angeles. We all met and had our eats on an outdoor patio. Then Kim's girlfriend shared about their church and, more specifically, how they approached the issue of romantic love and marriage. Their assembly believed in God-given matches and taught these principles to where they became a part of their church culture. This wasn't an exception but very normal for them. Over 100 couples had met and married by revelation from God and not by the American dating system so prevalent in our society. My ears perked up. This was the encouragement from the Lord I had been asking for! This was the confirmation that this was where God wanted me to be.

After a couple of hours, we hit the interstate, heading north once again for the Land of Lincoln. We conversed over what had been said over lunch, and even though we hadn't yet received detailed revelation on how to get to Music City, we got enough light from Jesus to confirm that Nashville was indeed calling us. This just meant that we would need to continue to trust through all that was not yet known and wait for the next step. I could speak for myself, and I know Kim would agree; we had a lot of experience doing that waiting thing, so let's do it some more!

With my career ending, there were delays that I didn't see coming. Nashville was the destination. It would be another two and a half years before the moving truck would pull out on Easter morning. Why the delay? Some very unexpected and vital things would happen first. That would be revealed in its own sweet time!

Back at the auto factory, everyone seemed to have a plan for what to do next. I remember walking out of the plant for the last time that cold and cloudy late November day while listening to what all my ex-co-workers were planning to do. Some had new jobs lined up, and a few had already begun working. The Federal Government offered 20k for school because we qualified under certain conditions. A lot of guys and girls took advantage of the gratuitous training. Many people were moving out of state, and other older co-workers threw in the towel and retired. For me, all I knew was that God had said Nashville was next. The only problem was that Nashville wasn't yet happening, and how I wished it would hurry up! This was going to take some kind of miracle. I was called to take an unheard-of concept music project to a city overloaded with musicians competing to be heard. No one knew me. I had no job contacts or any place to land in Tennessee. I listened for the next step, asking the Lord if I should take another job in Illinois while I waited...

crickets. This was the space in between, and it was uncomfortable, to say the least. So I continued to do all I knew: wait.

There was just no peace in starting another career job. I remained unemployed, living off severance. I was about to learn much about why I needed to be freed up. A year after the festival, my Dad took a turn for the worse and passed on to the next life. He had previously been in remission from leukemia, but the nasty disease came roaring back. At once, I headed to South Carolina and would need to be there for an extended period. Many people sent flowers and condolences for my father, as was the custom. My friend, Kim, sent me a bonsai tree that would live past the flowers that so quickly withered to honor my Dad. I thought it was a beautiful gesture. My mother, elderly herself, would now be in their house alone. I stayed with her for over a month to help with many things. My family dynamic had begun to change.

The summer of 2016 would be like none I had experienced. It was both joyful and difficult at the same time. While not working, free time was in abundance. Living by faith requires revelation, and until it comes, doing whatever you wish for the sake of it feels wrong. The pressure to invent something to do for myself was always whispering, but I knew that I would never produce the promises. I needed to have divine direction. Purpose-filled waiting can be one of the best things to do with your "nothingness". I continued to wait.

The year 2016 would also bring me an incredible thrill, one of a lifetime. I spent the entire summer driving through town and the surrounding area while listening to my Cubs on the radio. I had never listened to or watched as much baseball as I did that year. Any casual sports fan would know what a heartbreak the Chicago Cubs had been for decade upon decade. Each spring, the hope was, "Maybe this year." In 2016, I, along with millions of Cubs fans, would experience the most significant sports moment of our lives! The Cubs did nothing but win throughout the regular season. Having lived in Chicago, I'd been to dozens of games in the past. But this year of '16 was the first time I took in a night game at Wrigley. It was an extra long game. It was in the thirteenth inning when Pittsburgh took the lead. It looked as if the Cubs were going to drop this one. We left before the game ended, only to hear the Cubs come back and win in the bottom half of the inning. We missed it. It was that kind of year for the Cubbies. As the regular season came to a close, Chicago just ran away with the Central division.

The playoffs began, and the North Siders found victory in each round. Then, as the World Series played out, they trailed badly. I had been planted in front of a television for every game, but my friend Kim and I had tickets to see Christian metal giants Stryper in Indy on Saturday night. I would miss the game that evening. The show also included veterans Petra and Whitecross and a few local bands, so it was a long night of loud rock. Checking the score from time to time, the Cubbies were losing horribly. This loss meant they would trail three games to one in the series, odds almost impossible to overcome. They would need to win three in a row. I felt deflated.

Kim had previously shared a story with me of a reveal that God had given her years before I knew her. She was friends with a local high school athlete attending the same high school from which we both had graduated from. Our school was already state champions in football this year, and now the basketball team was heading into the state championship game. Then she said something that has stuck with me all this time. Kim told me that for His own reasons, God had revealed to her that our school would indeed bring home the championship trophy in hoops. In her mind, this was a done deal, but...the game still had to be played. That meant all the battles and drama that a game such as this brings would still have to occur. Kim purchased a money clip as a graduation gift for this young man and engraved it with the win date *before* the win happened. This would prove that she indeed heard Jesus ahead of time. The game was hard fought, and our old school hoisted the state championship trophy when it was over! It was only the second school in the entire state of Illinois to ever win both the football and basketball championships in the same year. Epic!

Once, I personally watched Kim inform a young lady at our church to go home and take a pregnancy test because God had revealed to her that she was about to have her second child. Nine months later, a baby boy was born! Jesus tells her these kinds of things.

Next, it seemed it was my turn because she said something that made me think she knew about the Chicago Cubs win ahead of time. I think she mistakenly gave away that the North Siders were destined to be World Champions. If I heard her right, it would take a miracle of sorts to be in order with Chicago down three games to one to Cleveland. There was no shortage of drama, nothing easy about it. The Cubs fought back and tied the series at three games each. It all came down to the final game. A good buddy who is a big Cubs fan invited me to his home to watch game seven on the big screen with his family. We were glued to the television. The North Siders had a good lead, but the Indians tied the game late. Extra innings, and then a rainstorm came. Delay. Finally, as things resumed, Chicago wasted no time and scored two runs, and Cleveland scored one. The Chicago Cubs were World Champions! It happened, we saw it, we experienced it, and it only took 108 years. We sat there speechless, emotionally spent, but thrilled beyond description. Nothing I would ever experience in the entire sports world would ever equal the 2016 Chicago Cubs.

My buddy, his kids , and I attended the Chicago celebration parade a few days later. The six-mile parade route was stuffed with over five million Cubs fans in a frenzy. One of the largest crowds ever to gather for a single event! I had never seen such a mass of Cubby blue in my life; it was breathtaking.

A few weeks passed when I finally confronted Kim. "You said something that made me think that you knew ahead of time that the Cubs would win the World Series. Is that true? Did Jesus tell you the Cubs were going to be World Champions?" Kim looked at me and confessed, "Yes, He did!"

I took a mental note. This girl really does hear from God! In rather unusual ways, at that.

The year 2016 would be the end of an era. Things were "concluding," if you will. All the Creator had instilled in me in my home state would soon be exiting. A God-ordained project was to be moved to a strange land among strange people. I was excited and equally nervous over all the unknown factors. The journey had taken so much longer than I could ever imagine. The remaining time I had left in Illinois felt flat and lifeless. I was waiting for my exodus. With the Cubs World Series triumph, there seemed to be something "spiritually significant" for me to glean. As it played out, from a time perspective, I was able to enjoy the entire season, unlike any other year before or afterward. That was the summer of the Cubbies. I had a unique sense that the Lord was granting me an experience to savor. Even if the Northsiders were to win more fall classics, nothing would equal this one! I was so glad that I was still a resident of Illinois when it all happened because I could share it with so many others.

Watch the documentary; you will see how much it meant to Chicago and Illinois. There was a parallel between the Cub's victory and where I was in life at this point. But I struggled to put a finger on it. It wasn't until the documentary was released that the picture became more apparent. Ben Zobrist, the series MVP, made a statement in his summary of the Cubs finally winning it all. "We knew it wouldn't be easy, but we never knew it would be this hard."

- K -

Hello Darkness, My Old Friend

Yep, another Stryper show was on the calendar right in the middle of the 2016 World Series game. Considering his beloved Cubs were so close to winning it for the first time in a century, I gave Gary an out. I knew this was a HUGE deal for him, but one thing you gotta know about Gary Elliot: He is a man of his word. He made a commitment to rock, and he was going to follow through. While we were driving, I told him a secret. I told him I asked God if He would make it possible for Gary to meet Michael Sweet, Stryper's lead vocalist/guitarist. He responded to me like that was a stretch, asking, "And how exactly do you think that is going to happen?" I said, "I don't know, but why not? We all have the same Father, right?" In my mind, it was no big deal for God.

They were playing at this multi-plex theater complex of sorts. It had some age to it, so it had some really cool architecture to admire. By the time we pulled in, a significant line had begun to form, so we hurried to get ourselves into place. Stryper stories were buzzing on all sides as fans shared out loud with one another. After about an hour of the line not moving, I catch a long-haired shadow out of the corner of my eye. I turned to focus, and whom do I see coming down the line? None other than Michael Sweet!

He was coming out to say hello. I see him pass by, catching people off guard as their brains try to catch up with what they see. Hardly anyone took advantage to chat. I poked Gary to get ready for what was coming our way. As he approached, I boldly stuck out my hand and introduced myself. He was super friendly and thanked us for coming out. Then he looked down behind me and asked, "So, what's that?" I looked down for something that had maybe dropped to the ground. He pointed more behind me, and I said, "Oh, this is my friend Gary." He said, "Hey. No, what's that on your wrist?" No joke, I had at least three inches of bracelets stacked on my wrist when I figured out he was pointing out my wrist tattoo: Jeremiah 33:3. I recited the scripture, "Call upon Me, and I will answer you and show you great and mighty things, things you've never considered before." Michael Sweet replied, "Cool, very cool!" And moved on.

I was super surprised that Gary didn't assert himself to an introduction, and I realized I should have done the honors; after all, I was the one who asked for the divine opportunity. Gary, who is covered in tattoos, started joking about Michael noticing my tiny wrist tattoo covered with three inches of bracelets and walking by his own prominent ink gallery starting from the neck down. The jokes got bigger and more ridiculous as the night went on.

We had a lot of fun, but there was one thing happening that I didn't disclose to him at that time. Once Michael Sweet walked off, my right hand, which he shook, began shaking off and on throughout the night. It was a peculiar experience to me but not unfamiliar. I've heard through different Christian channels that God can use such experiences to bring your attention to something He wants to say to you. So, right in the middle of the Stryper performance, I asked God what He wanted to say. I heard Him speak to my spirit to prepare to make an impact within the music industry, "No longer go to these events planning to be entertained but prepare to make an impact."

He was refining my call to dreamers down to dreamers in the music industry. Later, I would come across an interview with Brian Welch of Korn testifying of his mind-blowing transformation and God returning him back to the band that nearly destroyed him, only to bring proof of the transformation God did in him to the fans and the band. I always wanted to be the girl "with the band." Somehow, some way, I was heading back to the kind of backstage access I had back in the day with our local talent, only this time full of the power of a Holy God. What a joy!! My being in Nashville was starting to make even more sense. 2016 was turning out to be an outpouring of lining us up on purpose, a narrowing of our parallel lines.

At this point in our story, you probably wonder why Gary was not seeing it, too. You, me, and a handful of friends wondered the same thing. I would like to say I handled this, waiting for what I hoped to be, like a champ. I didn't. It was hard, and I'm not talking about uncontrollable attraction. I'm talking about believing what God said to me.

It was hard to live out faith in what you thought you heard while living everyday life out the exact opposite. I doubted, cried, and complained. I tried to feel out his insights on the many parallel lines we walked a couple of times, got tired, got sad, and wanted to quit. However, one thing I experienced was that God won't let you quit. Now, don't get me wrong. You can quit, but it won't be because God quit. He met my every cry, complaint, mistake, and fainting of soul with Himself and His words. God is smart. He knew every weakness that would surface within this impossible wait, and He had already prepared His responses and His timing to get the most honesty out of me. I had grown into one of the most determined daughters He had. I would get what God promised. He burned the quitter right out of me. I wanted nothing more than to add to His pleasure already cascading over me and with more of my trust in His goodness. I wanted out of this promise as much as I wanted to stay in it. I learned He was attracted to all my weaknesses along the way because He would be found strong in them.

God had said early on to not look at Gary as though there was something wrong with him and to not look at me as though there was something wrong with me. I initially thought, okay, cool. I didn't know then that He was setting up a living objective for the next four years! It wouldn't take long for me to begin to question the very questions God told me not to entertain. A divine plan that grew more evident to me by the year showed no signs of the obvious to Gary. I would get weak and default to those very questions God told me not to. What's wrong, why can't he see what I see? What's wrong with me that keeps him from being curious about me? What's wrong with me that I can't keep from wavering in my faith? The only response I would get from God was to remember what He said. I was not supposed to entertain the "what's wrong" kind of questions. I had to rely on greater truth to keep my eyes looking ahead.

I took these accusations captive every time they sounded off and countered them with scriptures that declared the truth about him. Gary was full of the same Holy Spirit as me. Jesus promised He would lead us into all truth. If He led me, He would lead Gary. The love of God abounded in Gary as it did me. The more I reinforced those truths, the more I became confident there was nothing wrong; there was only something missing—revelation. I was determined not to rob God of what Gary had waited for the longest to hear from Him and Him alone: "She's your wife." That was not my place, and I cherished that intimate privilege for both of them. I was determined not to tell him what God said to me but rather to keep His words to me as a confirmation of what God would soon be telling him. After all, we are encouraged in the Song of Solomon not to awaken love before its time because love has a time.

I had a history of hearing from God. Most of those times, I was right, and in all those times, I looked to be the fool until the moments before He proved His words. By this time in our story, all pride, lust, and selfish gain had been burnt out, and all I wanted was for God's words to "become flesh" in my life. I wanted His desires for me satisfied through me, and if His desires for me led to a different outcome than what I was expecting, I would be okay because I would be found faithful.

Gary and I would have conversations throughout our friendship, finding an agreement that there is a fine line between crazy and faith. Only time will reveal the difference. I lived those years anchored in the truth of John 16, "He [the Spirit] will guide you into all truth." Every time "crazy" would come knocking at my door, I'd hide myself in that truth over and over again.

The summer of 2016 was ramping up to be another threshold crossing for me and my daughter Andee. We were getting her ready to marry the boy next door. Literally, he lived next door. As mentioned before, God woke me in the middle of the night during the summer of what would become her senior year of high school and told me she would find love shortly after her senior year. She did. Andee never had to date around to find the one God had for her. She was his sister's best friend, which set up a sweet opportunity for them to come to know one another within a family atmosphere. He was intelligent, talented, kind, and noble.

We were renting the next-door house from his parents. It was the first time Andee and I got to live in a house of our own. We had been apartment dwellers throughout her years in school. When I first walked into the early 1900 bungalow, I was struck by all the windows and natural light. You don't know what you're missing until you step into it. It was the sweetest little nest with a fireplace, hardwood floors, and, guess what, a narrow unfinished staircase to a dimly lit attic. I thought I heard the Lord whisper that it would be a honeymoon suite. My dad came to see it shortly after we moved in, and he said it reminded him of the first house he and my mom lived in after their honeymoon. I took that as confirmation and teased Andee, "The first to get married gets to keep the "honeymoon" bungalow." It was funny until the day came when this boy next door, Zech, set up a surprise FRIENDS reenactment of Chandler and Monica's engagement in my front living room. A group of us were hiding in Andee's bedroom, just like in the show, waiting to overhear the romantic proposal so that we could burst in with a tearful celebration. Andee would get married six months later, and I would be the one moving out.

I had packed everything I owned and stored it in the basement. I let Zech and Andee use my living room furniture until they could get their own. I had reserved the most minimal things needed to live temporarily in Illinois alone until Nashville called. I remember preparing for Andee's wedding. There was so much divine provision and great innovation when they decided to get married in joining backyards. We recruited Gary to hand paint signs for the big day. He would come over a couple of times a week and work on them in the barn. Our friendship was strong and peaceful.

I was looking forward to having him at the wedding. He would have a profound understanding that most wouldn't, waiting years for a promised marriage only to see my daughter's promised marriage come first. Unfortunately, it was not meant to be. Gary's father passed right before her big day. I was feeling great sympathy for his loss, wishing I could be there to support him. He had been looking forward to supporting me in giving Andee away in marriage and had bought a special hat for the occasion. Even though Gary was not there in person, his hand-painted signs lined the event and added to the perfection of a beautiful evening.

Andee was stunning, and the peace she carried glowed on her. They were precious to watch, especially as she recited her vows. Zech responded by saying, "Thank you." We all giggled. My friend, Pastor Jeff, who had been a solid fatherly influence in Andee's teen years, got to marry them. The day was perfect. I was so happy for her and kind of numb to the reality of the transition. Our relationship would never be the same. We would no longer be Kim and Andee. It would be Zech and Andee, and my daily role was now moving into an "as-needed basis."

My best friends, Niki and Paula, well aware of what God had promised me over the years, were at my side helping me clean up and prepare that sweet little "honeymoon suite" for the kids' return. They helped me pack my car with the last bit of necessities for my next phase of waiting, about 40 minutes down the road in a tiny apartment in a tiny farm town. I remember getting into my car to leave. It was dark. It was quiet, and I was all alone. I turned the ignition, and the radio came on to Disturb's version of "The Sound of Silence" only a rocker could appreciate. Like an almost haunting holy invitation, I heard, "Hello, darkness, my old friend." It was as though God was inviting me to remember His faithfulness over the years to meet me in the dark, quiet places I did not expect to be going. It was an invitation for more of the same, waiting for the known within the unknown.

I drove away from that sweet little house, the last home I'd share with my daughter, walked into my new tiny apartment, turned on the bedroom light, and my phone went off. It was a text from my friend Gary asking how the day went and how I was doing. It was like me and Gary and Jesus were together in this new place. He was missing life with his father, and I was missing life with my daughter, sharing an important moment in time and space. The friend I knew he would have been for me in person was still that friend I needed at a distance. He followed up my response with the most fitting encouragement. My heart felt so strong. I had a good hard cry and got up to get dressed for bed. Out of the corner of my eye, I saw a piece of clothing or something sticking out from under the bed. I reached down to pull it up. It was a University of Tennessee ball cap left by the previous resident. As backward as my life appeared, moving into a promise, I knew I was in the right place at the right time, with Nashville, Tennessee still to come.

SCENE FIFTEEN:

3:34

- G -
I Couldn't Stop It!

THROUGH THE YEARS, I'D BEEN out with many girls since I had given up on the idea of dating. That may sound like a paradox, but it isn't. Dating when I was much younger was always connected to the romantic, trying to find love or maintain what I'd already had. It was all about me trying to make it happen for myself. Now, my time with the opposite sex was nothing of the sort. It was to bless them if I could, to enjoy them as sisters and have a little social fun at the same time. My trust for love was not in some societal system, a cultural ritual, but in the promise of God that He was going to match me, He was going to provide, and He was going to be true to His word. Yes, I was spending time with ladies on social outings now and again, but the motive of the heart was pure.

My severance from 26-plus years at the auto factory was about to run out. I landed a part-time gig driving a small bus for the mentally challenged to keep financially afloat. I would converse with Heaven daily while in the driver's seat. During those times, I would pray for my future wife, asking for God's hand to be at work in her life. These prayers had been voiced for decades. Also included was my request for God to send her. But on this particular Thursday in early May, the strangest thing occurred. I could no longer ask for God to send her. Like a clock striking Midnight, something felt finished, like the prayer was answered. Why? What God said decades earlier was in place now, "When these things come to an end, she will be found because I will present her to you. All I ask of you is to believe Me and rest." That new period of time had arrived. That request was no longer needed. Deep within, I knew that she was coming, and very soon. It was a done deal; game over. All I could do was thank God. As the clients were yelling at each other, as was typical, I heard none of it because Jesus and I were in the driver's seat celebrating!

Kim and I had grown into close friends, but friends only. Both of us loved loud, heavy music, so whenever an artist came around, we'd be there. Disturbed, Stryper, Quiet Riot, LA Guns, Plum, Petra vocalist John Schlitt, and a slew of local groups were some of whom we had gone to see. We enjoyed women's roller derby, classic cars, and movies. Kim and I would hang out once a month, twice at the most, sometimes in groups, other times just the two of us. I enjoyed her company and cherished her friendship.

As 2017 opened, something strange began to happen. Over time, I began to notice that I was thinking about Kim during my day, as I had never done before. It made me uncomfortable, to be honest. It would all fade until the next time we hung out together; it would happen all over again. We had been friends for four years. Why would she be dividing my attention now? I began to "resist" and "reprimand" such thoughts. But I couldn't control them. Surely, this was the devil playing tricks with my mind, and I was going to have none of it. I did my best to put this "demonic" nonsense behind me. Spiritual warfare was certainly needed! Onward soldier!

A longtime friend and I were going to meet Kim at her father's house, where she was living temporarily. The three of us were going to hike some trails by a large lake in the area. It was a beautiful early spring day, and we had a relaxing time. This draw to Kim was stronger than ever. It felt involuntary, and I couldn't stop it. There had been many crushes over the years, but I had never experienced a magnetism like this with another female. This was something beyond those silly crushes. Now, for the first time, I began to wonder if this was the Spirit of God in me.

- K -
TIME TO CHANGE THE SUBJECT

By this time, I had moved from my tiny apartment to my dad's house, still waiting for directions to Nashville. I was getting weary. I had been in temporary living situations for close to a year now. All my belongings remained in the basement of the sweet little "honeymoon" bungalow. There was no direction to leave for Nashville. There was no indication Gary was seeing me as more than his friend as he continued living in a house full of boxes packed for his own move to Nashville. I would search the internet for jobs and get sick to my stomach because God was not in it. I would make separate trips to Nashville for different occasions, hoping a door would open when I was there. It didn't. I remember walking the square in Franklin, TN, trying to imagine myself there, enjoying the new landscape, making new friends, and starting a new job. But God interrupted, "Why do you keep seeing yourself here alone?" I replied, "Because it's easier to believe I can get a job and move to Nashville alone than it is to believe Gary is going to see me as Your choice and marry me first." Some things we can do for ourselves, we think. Get our own jobs, rent or buy our own homes, and make our own friends. Who needs God for everyday life?

I never signed up for the "everyday life." I signed up for a life that could not be explained outside the Holy Spirit and got it. After that exchange, I was done looking to Nashville as a single. I would be going as a married woman or not going at all, end of story, and contentment took hold. Meanwhile, Gary, living amongst a pile of moving boxes, asked God for a job while waiting only for God to respond by pointing him to Nashville. Gary was expecting to move to Nashville single and then marry the one God had for him once he was there. Well, which was it, God?

Anybody who has walked out an unbelievable call from God will tell you they had several moments where they just wanted to give it back to Him. We all have our limits simply because our imaginations are limited. God said He will do above and beyond what we can think or imagine, right? Enough time can pass in the waiting when you wonder if you're crazy or if there is a way to get out of it. That was me. Nobody waits this long for a spouse! I was learning that God disagreed with my perceived limits.

Can I have a new call? Am I crazy? Can we just change the subject? That is precisely what I asked out loud to God, walking back to my desk one day. Within days, I noticed my faithful timing of "33" was changing. I caught the clocks and timers changing from "33" to "34" within a split second. This happened several times when I caught on that God might be saying something new. So I asked Him, "Why am I catching the number changing from "33" to "34"? He responded, "I'm getting ready to change the subject." I knew in my spirit that the prayer subject of my promised husband was about to be "checked" off my list of expectancies. I was strengthened to keep going just a little more. But why 34? Later, I found a journal entry in my journal dated Easter Sunday morning in 2016 as I was alone in that sweet bungalow, having couch time with Jesus, reading the Song of Solomon. I commented on chapter 3, verses 3-4, that I knew the time of revelation was drawing near. It read, "Scarcely had I passed them when I found the one my heart loves. I held him and would not let him go till I had brought him to my mother's house..." Revelation was coming.

ACT III

DID THE SUN COME OUT, OR DID YOU JUST SMILE AT ME?

SCENE SIXTEEN:

YOUR "WIFE" IS SPLENDID

- G -

Ratt and Roll!

T WAS TIME FOR ANOTHER rock show! That meant a road trip. Ratt was my favorite of all the bands that came out of the early Sunset Strip hair band era. In my mind, their song "Round and Round" was the song that defined that period the best. Ratt and Roll and Thursday was the night. Kim and I had tickets to see Ratt, and I was like a giddy teenager. The club held around 1,500 rowdies and was stuffed to the brim with a mix of older nostalgic rockers and younger fans who had gleaned their tastes from their parents' cassettes. What excellent parental skills! We had our tickets scanned and then shoved our way to get as close as possible without being rude.

Ratt sounded so good, tight, raunchy, and loud, just like 1984! I stood on a wheelchair ramp against a handrail, and Kim was slightly behind me. One hammered dude after another slithered down the ramp, brushing right against me. It was somewhat irritating. Then, the unexpected. In a flash, a mere instant, it all happened. Life as I knew it was about to be rearranged.

While the music was thundering, I was lost, carried away in my youth, when I felt a sudden and sharp elbow in my rib. Probably another hammered clown with too many Buds in his belly. This time, I was thoroughly irritated. At once, I whirled around to see who the perpetrator was. Where was he? To my surprise, there was no sloshed maniac. It was then that I saw her, really saw her. Kim was looking up at me with a sweet and beautiful smile. I had seen that smile a thousand times before, but this time, it was different; something more was behind her smile! At that moment, through all that noise, I heard a quiet and familiar whisper, "She is your wife. No one will love you like she will." I stood there astounded. Guitarist Warren DeMartini may as well have been playing a washboard. Stephen Pearcy could have just blown his nose for all I cared. I was lost in this revelation! An instant love washed over me for Kim; it was overwhelming. This love was like nothing I had experienced before. I knew this love in me was from God and not another schoolboy crush. This love was completely selfless. I wanted to bless Kim;

I desired to honor and serve her. I felt the eagerness to cover her and to give her what she had been longing for her entire adult life. I had no concern whatsoever about what was in it for me. This is the kind of heart that does not originate from the natural human part of us. This brand of love must originate from divine love.

Finally, I had heard. It jolted me. I was ruined. And there it was! Finally, after hearing "no" from God so many times through the years with different women, I heard that same familiar voice say, "Yes."

I did my absolute best to enjoy the remainder of the show. I was astounded at what had just happened. Afterward, Kim and I had a 90-minute drive home and had to be up early the following day. I said nothing to her about what had just occurred. I lay in bed that night and just stared at the ceiling. My only question was, "What do I do now?" I had been living in the expectation for a really long time that God would reveal His lady He had promised. Many times, I had imagined what it would be like, and now I knew it had really happened. Yet, I had no clue how to proceed. This wasn't the typical romantic flick where two people chase each other without divine involvement. The kind that makes all the girls cry and sells a lot of Raisinets. These types of examples were of no help. I needed to ask Jesus how and when to do this.

A couple of things were evidently clear to me now. I instantly loved Kim that night at the Ratt bash. She was the one whom God presented. Unlike four years ago over pizza, before this revelation, I couldn't say no to her this time. To do so would be nothing short of defiance, rebellion, and loss. All the effort and work I had put into writing, speaking, and related music would amount to nothing if I said no. Frankly, my call would be over. Why? It was all designed by God with Kim in mind. I was meant to move forward in partnership with Kim, for the purpose He had assigned to me. The life I had been preparing for would stall, nothing would progress. If I had said no, I may as well get another meaningless job and drift. That is no life I was interested in; it is not an option. Forget Nashville, too. She was what my heart wanted and what my destiny needed.

It just so happened that Kim and I had planned to attend a steampunk fest in a nearby city the following Saturday. I wondered if she picked up on what had happened to me on Thursday night. After all, this girl can be dangerous like that. You know, Jesus does tell her stuff. As the day progressed, I committed to keeping this all to myself until I heard God show me how to progress. After a couple of hours of walking the downtown area and observing all the subculture displays and activities, we opted for a break to catch our breath. Upon finding a park bench in the shade, Kim and I planted ourselves down for a while.

An elderly man had a seat beside us. It was pretty evident that he had already been tilting the suds. He was emitting strong fumes of brew. We made some small talk for a short while when the man leaned over to me and declared of all things, "Sir, I must tell you that your wife is splendid!" What was that all about? Was God speaking, dropping hints through this half-blitzed dude at an underground culture event? I was unwilling to show my cards, so I simply replied that we were only friends. But I knew that wasn't really true any longer. But for now, I had to wear my poker face.

Later, after leaving the steampunk gig, we did a bit of shopping and then drove to meet up with a group of friends at a park, followed by a stop for frozen yogurt. It was dark now, and Kim had a long drive to her father's house. We left the others, calling it a night while they were still licking their frozen fun. Now, I found it difficult to sit still at home, so I went on a late-night walk to ask Jesus again what was next. There was no specific answer yet, but I sensed a great peace. He knew what He was doing.

Sunday would be a different story. I had told no one of the revelations received, but that was about to change. Midnight Valentine had asked a great friend, Mike, to oversee the band as pastor. Previously, He had been the pastor of a local church where I used to be involved. When Mike's church disbanded, I suggested that he consider Nashville. He did, and without hesitation, he went. Mike had already been in Nashville for a year or so by this time.

The idea of calling him and asking his counsel on how to move forward crossed my mind. I had just picked up the phone to make the call when I received a text from none other than Kim. She sent me a picture she had taken at the Ratt show on Thursday evening. The photo was my silhouetted profile, watching Stephen Pearcy singing and grooving in the distance, snapped at the very instant the Spirit of God revealed her to me as my wife. Can you say perfect timing? I recall hearing Kim taking some shots behind me that night, but she didn't know the significance of this one specific picture would hold. When I saw this picture glowing on my device, another whisper became clear, "You have waited decades for this; there is no more reason to hesitate. Now is the time. Tell Kim what I have revealed to you." I had my answer but called Mike for prayer nevertheless. I told him Jesus had revealed Kim as the one He had chosen for me. Mike was thrilled and prayed for God's peace over me. I texted Kim to see if she was free to meet before church at 6 p.m. She would be at my house at 3 p.m.

Mike's prayers were answered. I was calm, not nervous in the least. Kim arrived on time. We piled into my little car and drove north of town to a pavilion in a park. When she questioned what this was about, all I said was, "Jesus has messed me up, and now I'm going to mess you up." I'm sure that was of no help to her. It was then that I knew she had no clue what had happened in the last few days. The two of us planted ourselves at a picnic table. I made some worthless and silly comments about the couple playing tennis next to us and the overweight squirrels chasing each other. Illinois grows their squirrels plump and round with the abundance of corn. Then I decided I might as well just get to it. "Kim, Jesus has shown up, and He has spoken to me. Jesus has said that you are the one I've been waiting for. There is no other for me. It happened Thursday night when we saw Ratt. I've been a wreck for the last four days. Let's get married!"

And there it was! We talked more about what had happened Thursday night. Then she opened up and shared what she had been living with for the last four years. I hadn't a clue that Kim had been carrying such an element of faith. This level of faith wasn't for wimps. To wait in expectation the way she did and for this long couldn't be because I was such a great dude. No, in order for Kim to endure four years of hope with no evidence of anything happening was because she had heard from God. I was never her focus. The centrality of her gaze was Jesus. Kim wasn't waiting on me. The girl was waiting on and with her God. And now I was thrilled to deliver the news that He had been faithful to her! We stood up, got in a big hug, and left the park, newly engaged.

There were many things that God weaved into our story that took on miraculous dimensions. We experienced Him pulling tricks out of His hat to astonish us again and again. Later, when we remembered that afternoon among the chubby squirrels and green tennis balls, I recalled Kim's experiences with the number 3:33 changing to 3:34. These had been numbers that God had been revealing to her for a very long time. While we had paid no attention to the clock on the wall in the park, we retraced our steps from that afternoon. We met at my house at 3 p.m., then drove for 15 minutes to the park on the city's north end. After walking to the pavilion and engaging in small talk for a short time, I began to share the revelations of four days ago. All this to declare that Kim and I became engaged to be married at precisely 3:34 that Sunday afternoon! Miraculous!

SCENE SEVENTEEN

YOU'LL LOVE ME AT ONCE

- K -

1,000 Tears Over 1,000 Years

I LOVED WHEN GARY WROTE, "I wondered if she picked up on what had happened to me on Thursday night..." Um, no! The guy has an incredible poker face. The night before the concert, I had not slept. I was experiencing great wrestling within my spirit over all of this. I met up with Gary for tacos before the show. I told him I had not slept and may not be very energetic. He told me we could cancel. I almost took him up on it. Looking back now, I see the spiritual warfare taking place the night before to keep me from going to the Ratt concert with him.

I remember how cramped the venue was, hot and packed. We picked a high-traffic area to stand, which lent to the constant pushing and shoving as people tried to pass by us. I remember taking pictures with my phone and trying to line up Gary's profile from behind with the lead singer on stage. My plan was to tease him later that I had gotten his picture with Steven Pearcy. I remember driving home after the show, and there was not one thing about Gary's behavior telling of his earth-shattering revelation. I remember meeting up for the Steampunk festival and the friendly neighborhood drunk calling me Gary's wife. I also remember him making an unusual compliment about my legs. The compliment was not unusual. The fact that he was complimenting my legs was unusual. I remember catching him happily staring at me that night at the frozen yogurt place and calling his vocalist outside to talk before we left. I learned later that he was giving him an unspoken prayer request over his new revelation. I remember him being sweeter and kinder than usual as I left for my dad's house. None of this encouraged me; it puzzled me. I just thought it was weird.

That Sunday morning, I found the picture on my phone. I went for a long bike ride, and God revealed to me that He spared Gary from wasting his talent in his young adult years on raunchy cheap rock venues like many of the bands in his youth, but he *can* expect their kind of success with what God had given him to do. God had been preserving Gary's talent and influence for such a time as Nashville would provide. I was so excited for him that I texted the picture with that encouragement.

His only response was, "Can you meet me at my place before church at 3?" I had come to know Gary well enough that if I asked why he wouldn't tell me, he'd just restate his request. He leans toward the mysterious, and it's an endearing quality of his I don't mind indulging.

The closer I got to town, the more my mind spun with "what ifs." The only two things I could imagine he would want to take special time out to tell me was either he was finally moving to Nashville without me, or he found his wife, and it wasn't me. Clearly, I was not expecting his news to favor me. I got to his house just as he was coming out. He said to get in his car, so I did. I asked him where we were heading. He said I would see soon enough. There's that endearing, mysterious personality again. He was quiet, so I started to recount the weekend to make conversation as he drove. When we arrived at the park, he turned the car off and said, "Come on, Jesus had done messed me up, and I'm about to mess you up." Now I'm wide-eyed, quiet, and starting to brace my heart.

I went to the bathroom and grabbed some tissues in case a goodbye was coming. I sat across from him at a picnic table under the park's pavilion near the tennis courts. He started small talk about tennis and the ways of squirrels as the resident squirrels entertained us. This continued until I decided to stop asking the questions that were extending the small talk. He clears his throat and tells me he is not exactly sure how to say this, so he's just going to say it: "Kim, God told me you are the one." Have you ever heard the term "shock and awe"? That was me sitting across from him, stunned. It was just like my favorite childhood song in

Sleeping Beauty, "Once Upon a Dream": "...you (he) loved me at once..."
My first response was, "When?" He replied, "At the Ratt concert." "Four
days ago?!" I questioned. Then, he went on to rehearse the events of that
night. He then went on to list all the virtues he *loved* about me. I never
thought he had even been paying attention. Who was this guy? What
happened to my friend, Gary? Then, in all humility, he commented on
how he expected I would need some time to consider all that he had said.

I responded to him just as God had set me up to do many,
many months ago when I was walking through my kitchen, and out of
nowhere He spoke to my spirit to not delay my yes to him. So, I did not
delay in saying yes and I unfolded all that God had been speaking to me
over the past four years concerning him. Guess who was caught in shock
and awe, then?

Neither of us had a clue how to move forward from this
announcement until it dawned on me, "Hey, this means I get to finally
flirt with you!" He laughed, "Flirt away!" We hugged for the first time like
an engaged couple. We held hands for the first time, and all the new
sensations were so overwhelming. We got in the car, planning to grab
something to eat before church, but instead, we drove around town for
over an hour, processing out loud all that was happening and thinking of
all the people who were not going to believe this and all the people who
were going to be thrilled.

Our minds were spinning to catch up with what we knew in
our spirits. And we couldn't stop holding hands. Both of us, admitting we

did not have an appetite, resolved to go to his place to hang out until church started that night. He took me inside. We sat on the couch together. He wrapped his arm around me, and I nested into his broad shoulders. I heard my new fiancé pray over us as a couple, an engaged couple dedicated to God and one another to love.

So many people date to know whom they want to marry. They put their faith in all the information they learned and experienced with each other and move forward without hearing from their Creator Father. Our faith was in His words to us. Our yes to one another was first rooted in our yes to God for one another. The anchoring of faith in our marriage was now immovable. Our compatibility was obvious, which made us great friends but not yet spouses. Our attraction for one another arrived at different times, but we both knew attraction was not God's voice. We waited past compatibilities and attractions until our Father's voice said, "This is the one." Just like an Elliot!

I got back into my car to meet up with him at church. It was just me and Jesus and this incredible new life I stepped into. I could not catch up with one thought racing through my head when I suddenly experienced an incredible sensation of being clean. I had not sensed the presence of His holiness like that since I was first saved. I couldn't get over how clean I felt. Blessed are the pure in heart, those who only want what He wants, for they shall see God, and boy did I. I saw God move in the most profound way. It had to be a sensation of His pleasure in our faith. He said it was impossible to pleasure His heart without faith. It was clear that was exactly what our faith in His romantic ways did for His heart. Who were we to move His heart? We were His, and He was ours, trusting Him to do what He loves to do: join together His choices for love.

Gary and I did our best to behave ourselves during church that night. After the service, I got into my car and headed to see Andee. It was important to me that she would be the first I told. It was her one-year anniversary, and I texted her that I had an anniversary present for them. When I walked in, they looked at my hands to see where the gift was. I stalled a bit and said, "Well, I don't know how to tell you, so I'm just going to say it: God told Gary I'm the one." Andee's face went into shock, and then the tears started. She clung to me and cried. Zech was rubbing her back, saying how great this was. She cried even harder, and he said, "It is good, right?" I said, "Oh yes, this is what it looks like when decades of prayers are finally answered." It was a remarkable moment, the shedding of 1,000 tears over what felt like a wait of 1,000 years.

- G -

Mysterious Gift

A few years earlier, a group of friends had plans to celebrate my birthday. A couple of activities were scheduled for the evening, the first being a nice dinner at my favorite Italian eatery. A big problem, though, it was early February, and the weather had taken a turn for the worse. Freezing rain was making the city streets treacherous. And if that wasn't enough, the forecast predicted that the weather was going to get even worse. Yuk. It just wasn't safe to be driving out and about. That being the case, only a handful of friends were able to come to my birthday outing that evening, and I really didn't blame those who didn't make it. Nevertheless, those of us who did brave the elements hit the Italian restaurant, and then it would be onto some late-night bowling. Lighthearted, nothing too extravagant. All in all, the evening was still a lot of fun despite the smaller group.

Due to the weather, we called it a night early. While braving the stinging raindrops eager to morph into ice, Kim yelled at me across the parking lot. She informed me that she had gotten me something. I must admit that I wasn't comfortable with the idea, but I met her as she dug into the trunk of her car anyway. She pulled out a sizable box and handed it to me. Kim said something unusual, "This isn't a typical birthday gift; in fact, it's got nothing to do with your birthday. This probably sounds weird, but I bought this simply because Jesus told me to do so. I don't really know what it means and will leave that up to you and Jesus; He can tell you." Man, what does a dude make of this? I stuffed the box into my backseat, and each of us headed home before the streets turned into a skating rink.

Bursting in the front door, I shook the snow off myself as the temps had dropped, making snow from the rain. It was just a foul and nasty night. Placing the box on the table, I searched for a knife with which to open it. What could this be? After slicing open the top, I dug through wads of tissue paper and eventually pulled out a miniature ornate top hat. Hmmm… For the life of me, I had no clue what significance this could have. On my birthday, it was a mysterious non-birthday gift. But I had to admit it was a pretty cool decoration. I had a history with top hats, though. I'm not sure if Kim was aware that I played in a theatrical goth band not all that long ago. As I've said, we took underground subculture fashion very seriously, and to go along with my 6-inch platforms was one of my signature pieces, a felt top hat, a radical statement! So, in that sense, the decoration seemed very appropriate. But that still seemed like a stretch.

So, according to Kim's instructions, I questioned Heaven for what this meant. Maybe it held some secret meaning, or perhaps my friend, Kim, was a little on the lunatic side. Either way, for the time, there was no answer. After thanking Kim, I placed the ornate little hat on a shelf where I couldn't help but see it every day. It sat there for a very long time. Every so often, I would whisper to Jesus if this decoration held some hidden significance…crickets.

Why would God have her purchase this? Nevertheless, I continued to enjoy the top hat as it remained perched high on the shelf.

Once outside the metro Chicago area, or any other city in Illinois for that matter, the scenery is restricted to endless miles of cornfields. It looks all the same. I recall riding on highways through those fields for the first time with my new fiancé. We hadn't been engaged for an entire week as of yet. We had left town and were heading toward Kim's father's house in a rural area outside of a small town.

By this time, we had agreed on a wedding date and laid out some rough plans; we knew we wanted our wedding to be an artsy and unique experience. Something with a fairytale feel seemed appropriate because we saw the story Jesus had written for us as very storybook-like. There would be some whimsical trees and overgrown violets and glowing lanterns with vines made to mimic an enchanted forest, setting the mood. A massive clock would hang in the midst of the trees, frozen on the time of 3:34. We planned to read vows from a scroll. We both laid out a condensed version of our story of what Heaven did onto a twelve-minute video that was to play before the actual ceremony would kick off. Everything we did would hold deep symbolism. Kim actually came up with the idea that I would wear a custom-made purple suit jacket. Pinned to the lapel would be the casing of a pocket watch with a small violet enclosed. Then, for the finishing touch, my wedding attire would be a classy black felt top hat. You'd have to admit that you wouldn't see too many weddings like ours! And that's just the way we wanted it.

As we drove, I received a divine revelation three years in the making. From nowhere, the Spirit of God suddenly brought to mind the gift of that ornate little top hat that Kim had bought me when we were only friends. These are the words that came to me: "The miniature top hat I had Kim buy for you was My deposit securing your fairytale wedding." Who knew at the time that there would be a wedding but God? Who knew it would be a fairytale as such but the Almighty? And then, who knew that the groom would be wearing a top hat of his own that evening but God Almighty? He's brilliant like that! The wedding was taking on a story of its own.

SCENE EIGHTEEN:

WHEN YOUR FAITH IS JUSTIFIED

- K -
God Had Us in Mind All Along

I KNOW YOU / I WALKED WITH you once upon a dream /… You'll love me at once / the way you did once upon a dream. (Once Upon a Dream Songwriters: Sammy Fain / Jack LawrenceOnce Upon a Dream lyrics © Walt Disney Music Company). I married the man of a literal dream, the dream I dreamed so many years before I actually met him. My son-in-law, Zech, and I discussed the significance of that "frat house" dream. At first, that dream was used to comfort me, knowing there was a man who would be a desire of my heart and I could rest until he woke. Laying at the foot of his bed assured me, like in the book of Ruth, he would not miss me as if I had been lying at his feet. However, once my relationship with Gary came to pass, I got to see more of its meaning with him and my son-in-law.

We all agreed that the two hallways lined with the doors I passed by reflected the culture's ways of romantic pursuits. Ways driven mainly by self-interest and lust evolving into all kinds of perversions that the bodies and emotions of men and women were never created to experience and endure. Gary had two relationships he was ready to marry into that ended in heartbreak. His drive was his own then; it was not faith because faith rests, which is where I find him in the dream, resting.

It was as though I passed through hallways of Gary's history in resisting the spirits of the age. He knew there was a better way, a deeper rhapsody awaiting his soul than what was happening behind those doors. The more he dug into God's truth, the more he resisted, the more he rested above it all. The Bible lying open across his lap empowered him to believe. The man God had hidden in Christ, like me, was a soldier refined in the fires of God's desires for him. When I found him, he was no longer searching through the doors of the culture's ways to love, no longer fighting for his own ways but completely at rest.

As for me, my humility was on display by bending low to enter the narrow, unfinished staircase. I not only resisted those same spirits, but I walked a narrow path in friendship with Gary until he heard for himself what he had been waiting decades to hear: His Father's voice. My climb was steep and dimly lit, but the presence of peace and the immediate insight I had to rest at the foot of the bed until the time came was the fruit of my own intimate experience with God, grounded in my confidence in His voice like no other time in my life. God not only had a husband for me, but He had a man of daring faith with a history of life-shaping victories. Staying in my lane until Gary "woke" to His Father's voice, in turn, gave Gary the confidence that I was not only going to be a wife who loved him but a wife who would honor him. Unlike all the other women he encountered before me, I was the one woman shaped by the fires of waiting to wait with him for the many impossible things yet to come.

It was Friday, the end of the work week. I had been engaged for five days! However, this morning, I woke up with Mom on my mind. I had come to understand her wedding ring set, the one I never had a release to give up, was God saving it for my own wedding after all. I had a sweet encounter one night looking at it. The light had bounced off one of the glittering diamond pieces into a blue reflection that stirred a childhood memory of being a little girl, playing dress-up with my mother's jeweled wedding veil. In a moment, my heart changed, and I could no longer live without the ring set I had first considered pawning off. God revealed to me that the missing center diamond would be coming from my husband and will always serve as a testimony of his revelation of God's ways in the romantic, resting in my revelations of

God's ways in the romantic. Not just two people becoming one but two parallel stories finally crossing over into one.

I was deeply missing my mom, her laugh, her bright smile, her delight in me, and her faith for this day. This was the event she heard about from our Father: "There will be a man who will hear My voice." This was the event she died still believing for. This was the event she requested that deep violet amethyst pendant to celebrate. For the first time, I saw that what she gave back to me in that pendant was meant to be a token of her faith to take into my wedding. By letting me pick it out for her she froze a moment in time with me and secured an element of her love and desire for this very day. I could hardly believe it. God had that pendant planned for this very moment in time. It was as if I could hear eternity joining in on the celebration. Faith is eternal! It lives on far past our bodies. Faith is a substance of things hoped for and never passes away, never returns void. I knew I had to find a dress with a neckline that framed it best. Needless to say, I was weepy all day with the sweet and brilliant way God made sure to weave my mom into my wedding day.

I couldn't wait to tell Gary about my morning. As we drove through the cornfields to my dad's that evening, he called his mom so that we could meet for the first time. Shelby Jean had one of the sweetest Southern voices I'd ever heard. She had just enough spice in her spirit that I knew we'd have all kinds of fun, mainly at Gary's expense. After our call, I began to tell Gary about my morning with the Lord, the wedding set, and the amethyst pendant. He was super attentive. I told him all about shopping for the pendant with my mom and how God lined it up so that I would have a memorial of her faith to wear at the wedding. As I told him I would be wearing it on our wedding day, he interrupted, "Kim, that's my birthstone." We both just stared at each other. I abruptly barked, "STOP IT!" How could this be? God surprised us both with this one. Purple violets pointing to my someday wedding, and now a purple gemstone pointing to my someday fiancé? Who could write this kind of stuff up? Only God. There is no greater author of love.

The following five months were a whirlwind of first kisses, moving my daughter and her husband to Nashville, me moving back into that sweet little nest of a honeymoon bungalow, date nights, fairytale wedding preparations, kisses, moving Gary's stuff into the basement, learning each other with lots of laughs and more kissing, and meeting Gary's family all leading right up to our wedding day—my birthday, of course. Four years to the day we were first introduced. The provision and the peace were incredible throughout that whole time. There was not one stressful moment throughout. It was as if grace came like a wave and carried us into the day God had already written.

- G -

An Unusual Path

The day had come, November 17th—wedding day! Typical for Illinois, it was cold and windy. You know it's easy to get caught up in how you think an event will occur by repeatedly rehearsing it in your mind. It seems that when we get caught away in those things, it all moves in slow motion. Instead, the real thing was surreal. The day went by so fast that it was almost a blur.

The morning and early afternoon were full of visiting with friends and family. There was an excellent breakfast with my mother and sister up from Carolina and a mid-day meal with some buddies. It was good to share part of my day with them. I went home for a couple of hours of alone time. Then, late afternoon had arrived, and I was due at the church. Kim's inspiration for our wedding was *Alice in Wonderland*. From the eyes of the world, we were "mad" to believe in divine matches the way we did, especially as long as we did. This theme fits us perfectly! The church looked more like the set of a play than it did a traditional wedding. It could have been mistaken for a Burton production. Weddinggoers were in for quite a surprise when they entered the sanctuary.

All preparations were in line, and then we had photographs taken. Then the time had arrived; this was it! I walked my mother down the center aisle and seated her in the front row, boldly in my vivid violet coat, chartreuse silk ascot, and black felt top hat. I exited stage left as the artsy video started to tell the tale of how the Creator made our match. It was a much-condensed version of this very book. Our desire in all of this was for people to know that God still writes love stories, perhaps even for them.

I waited in the hallway while the video concluded and then took center stage with Pastor Jeff. Music filled the room, and Kim walked the aisle she had waited to walk for so long. It was the aisle of the church building she had discovered and named. She glowed while holding her father's arm, she was a sight to behold! It was a treat for me to watch her, especially from my perspective. Kim joined me, and the three of us stood before the congregation. Kim's ol' rock band buddy and pastor, Jeff, resided over our nuptials. Jeff had seen firsthand the level of faith Kim had displayed in the world of the romantic. Through all the struggles, lies, and hardships, the girl would not let go of the conviction that her God would provide His best for her.

Marriage came much later than Kim and everyone else in her corner anticipated, so much so that some who used to believe along with her fell off the banana boat. "Nope, she missed it," they said. "Somewhere in this process, everything went South. It looks as if there will be no husband for Kim after all. The girl waited too long, and romance passed her by. Maybe she is a bit on the wacky side in all this fairy tale belief?" Jeff was one of those who initially believed with Kim but seemed to waver as time marched on. And to our complete surprise, one of the first things out of Jeff's mouth to all the weddinggoers was to apologize publicly to his friend, Kim, for not believing for the duration with her. Not that she was seeking vindication from anyone, but she got it nonetheless.

I had some of the same experiences with peers of my own. My longtime friend, Kelly, had heard me teach on divine matches many times. She also knew that I had a promise from Heaven that I would receive God's best in a wife. Kelly is a dynamic woman of faith, and when I would make these claims, she would hear the faith behind them and agree. Kelly was on my side! I know that the girl was happy for me when I stood with confidence that Heaven could be trusted to this level. The issue was that over time, when there was no evidence of this developing in my existence, Kelly forgot the revelation that I was hanging my hat on, and she simply filed my name in the "forever single" file.

It was a hot August evening, and the countdown to November 17th was well on its way. We were hard at work preparing for our wedding with only a few months left. A buddy of mine and I walked into the home improvement store to purchase materials to manufacture our whimsical trees. Construction was waiting. Down aisle 11, we ran into Howard, whom I hadn't seen since his wedding many years earlier. We caught up on things when Howard finally asked us what we were working on. "How do I explain this...we are constructing props, whimsical trees," I replied. Howard looked down at our cart full of heavy sheets of foam. "Oh, I get it...for a play?" Howard reasoned. I shook my head, "Not quite; these fairy tale trees are for a wedding, my wedding." Howard's mouth hung open. He could not believe that I was getting married. Just like Kelly, he knew what I believed in the romantic arena. I had been rather vocal about it in the church where I first met Howard. As time passed, everything I proclaimed back then must not have stuck. Howard considered me a member of the "lifetime singles society."

My mother (who has since passed) was one of my biggest supporters when I began writing on God-ordained love. She was a fan! Yet when it came time to apply this message to me, she wavered as time passed. I had voiced my promise from the Heavens to her as well as to my father before he died. She was all on board with having a daughter-in-law and joined her faith with mine. But by the time I reached my upper 40s, I could hear a tinge of panic in her voice. Ma was growing fearful that I would go to the grave all alone, never walking the aisle of matrimony. Occasionally, she would voice her concern in her sweet Virginia way. I was completely at rest with no worries or concerns whatsoever. Finally, I told her, "Ma, you are much more worried about this than I am. Relax." So, I'll never forget the excitement in her voice when I shared the news over the phone that I was engaged. I couldn't tell for sure, but I think I heard her dancing in the background!

So Jeff, Kelly, Howard, and my dear mother were stunned out of their wavering belief when hearing the news that God was completely faithful, even after all those years. But what about the doubt that eventually came to haunt them? And at the end of the day, what about their unbelief? Why didn't they endure in faith? I believe these people wavered off-center simply because it wasn't their personal promise. While they fed off the belief I displayed for a time, that only went so far.

Each drifted in the long haul because God had spoken and confirmed my promise to me and not to them. A God-ordained love was my revelation and not theirs.

Now that Pastor Jeff had rid himself of his guilt, it was on to the rest of the wedding. Everyone joined in as we sang a beautiful worship song. We heard another song accompanied by an acoustic guitar and violin; we took communion with our friend, Mike, who came in from Nashville while weddinggoers joined us. Then, it was time for our vows. Keeping with the fairytale theme, we read our promises from a scroll. Jeff then announced us as husband and wife! And on the spur of the moment, an idea hit me. We leaned in for the traditional first kiss as a married couple; I peeled off my ornate top hat and held it in front, hiding the kiss from the crowd. No one expected that, not even Kim. We stepped down, walked the aisle, and out of the sanctuary to wonderful applause!

And just like that, it was over.

Now I understand why wedding celebrations go on for much more than an hour in Jewish tradition. While I was looking forward to beginning married life, I somehow wished we could have slowed this roll down and lingered here in wedding mode for a time. This was to be a once-in-a-lifetime event; let's hang out and enjoy this for what it is!

Sometime later, after we had settled into our new life together, I was in a reflective mood. I recalled the first prayer I prayed way back at summer camp, asking Jesus for the girl He would have for me. I was only 18 years of age. You know He heard that prayer. Little did I know that the answer would come 38 years later. If you had asked me as a teen if I would be willing to endure just short of four decades, would I have still prayed to the Heavens? I don't know, but in His wisdom, Jesus only asks you to trust Him one day at a time. What an unusual path. Nevertheless, I wouldn't have had it any other way!

SCENE NINETEEN:

BEAUTIFUL VENGEANCE

- K -

Beal Bourbon Broadway and Back to Beal

I T WAS AN A-LINE WHITE gown with lace overlay and delicate sheer long sleeves. The neckline was a deep V, providing the perfect nesting frame for the deep violet tear-shaped amethyst pendant to rest as I walked the aisle to the one who heard God's voice.

Gary slipped the 1.2-carat princess-cut Canary Yellow diamond (resting within my mom's wedding set) onto my finger, a wedding ring we designed together. I became fascinated with yellow diamonds when I witnessed my first one shopping with Andee for her dream wedding ring. Fascinating was the perfect word to describe my love for Gary. It was not only a symbol of our unending love for one another but a declaration of God's providence setting us up—a forever reminder of what God Himself put together. Gary's divine revelation of God-given love resting within mine, which first belonged to my mom, now our faith intertwined, telling a profoundly enchanting love story only God could write. And then he took it off, turned it around, and slipped it back on again. He had actually studied which side of the ring faces the heart. As he corrected course, he sent our guests into laughter, declaring, "This *is* my first rodeo, you know."

It happened! It really happened. God spoke His words, found agreement, and it became flesh after 25 years. He brought him to my door as I asked. Ok, it was a church door but it was *my* church door nonetheless. I have never felt more confident hearing God's voice than I did the day Gary heard I was his wife from God. However, it was not gained in a day; it grew throughout decades of contradiction.

I am going to open up my journal to you for a more intimate understanding of what it feels like at times to have a promise, yet all of life around you contradicts it. It was 2012. I had been believing God for 20 years. At this point, I had been distracted in my thoughts with the Dead Marshes out of *Lord of the Rings*. The Dead Marshes is the ancient battlefield of the Battle of Dagorlad between the Last Alliance and the forces of Mordor, where many of the fallen lay resting right where they fell in battle. Over time, the battlefield became marshes, swallowing up the dead. Decades after the battle, their bodies could still be seen floating face-up in the marsh waters.

This particular battle was the battle that closed out the second age, where the race of men defeated Sauron by cutting off his finger that held the Ring of Power. It was man's most significant victory, to finally undo the evil that had terrorized Middle Earth for centuries. However, man, too, desired power above all things and fooled himself into thinking he could yield its power. It would be thousands of years before the ring fell into the most innocent of hands to return to the fires that finally forged it.

Frodo, of the hobbit race, is the innocent one who crosses the Dead Marshes on his journey to return the ring. The battlefield, where thousands of the defeated lay underwater face up, reminds the onlooker of what was. Frodo's own defeat was awaiting him. For if he looked upon the defeated too long, he could become entranced and fall into the waters of their same defeat and join the dead. A journal entry from January 2, 2012:

I've known this past year was about working in a place that was not fit for me. I knew I was revisiting previous "battlefields" where the enemy holds me captive no more. Yes, I have been passing over the "Dead Marshes" of many historic personal defeats and disappointments. I've seen the faces of past enemies, disappointments, and false starts. If I stare at them for too long, I begin to become entranced by those memories, memories reinforcing my fears that this journey may lead to nowhere after all. What if all I'm doing is walking in circles of unanswered prayers? Lost forever without real purpose, no longer burning with the dream because it has been too hard for too long. It is taking everything He has given me not to fall face-first into the dead faces of defeat I see beneath my feet. It is taking everything He has given me to avoid the pull of death that is promising me relief. It's not exactly that I want to quit; I just can't continue roaming around this cemetery of the past while my soul is demanding a reward, a harvest, a breakthrough of answered prayers.

The faces told stories of aloneness, purposelessness, self-hate, and quitting. I have been believing in the impossible for over 20 years, and their faces stare up at me, suggesting He may never answer these desires on this side of Heaven. I would have despaired if I had not believed in the goodness of the Lord in the land of the living, so I keep walking, but it's so quiet, so lonely, and so dismal. I've become so gun-shy over every encouragement, as though I've heard it all before. I need something new, a new landscape, maybe a new dream because maybe I'm not who I need to be, maybe I'm not passing the tests, maybe I've got it all wrong. But I've seen too much now to consider those doubts for very long. He must come for me because one thing I do know is that He loves me with a relentless passion.

The only unbelief I seem to wrestle with is that God, All-Powerful, All-Knowing, Always-Present, Faithful, Author of my faith and my dreams, Convincer of truth, has not answered our desires by now. And they are our desires. I burn with what He desires. The two of us are in agreement. With all of my "yes's" added to all of His Sovereignty, it has become unbelievable to me that we haven't seen the fruit of our labors of great faith.

Is this the wilderness marking my heart never to forget Him in my future prosperity? Is this a test proving my faith? Or did I sell my inheritance for soup? I miss feeling in love with Jesus. It seems it was better for me back there. I pray that this is just a walk through the

Valley of the Shadow of Death and that the love will return better than ever before.

Working in the slave camps (of retail), knowing I'm not a slave, is a tension I fear I am giving into because the wait is too long for me now. Working this work without a word as a divine assignment shuts down all hope, creativity, and passion. Faith is hindered, prayers are unanswered, prosperity is strangled, and depression is graying everything.

Staring at walls, my four walls, and me. Deafening silence bounces from one wall to another. There is no dialogue but the single voice, your voice, wondering in your head. Wondering if you've been forgotten. Wondering if you've gone wrong. Wondering if too much time has passed. Wondering if your faith is just foolishness. Day after day after day passes you by as if you don't exist, as if the only future you have left is to wait for an ordinary end to what was planned to be an ordinary life after all.

You sit in the stillness of your life and wonder, "If I sit here, empty of all passion, would He come and break through to me?" I've done it. I've sat for an entire day in my own emptiness, exerting no efforts to know Him or to engage others. The result was nothing— another day alone like the last one. When interruptions to my stillness come, it's for their own good. They need what I have to give. I gladly give what I have, and I'm left right where I was before the interruption: alone. It's so empty an exchange to give what is needed and have no one to fall into that is simply there to love the likes of me. For wonderful revelation, they come for the asking. Encouraged and believing they leave. But I am left alone with much admiration and grateful goodbyes. The reward of service is so fleeting to me. To be pursued for your gifts alone is such an empty exchange. Awakened is the desire to be pursued for the joy of knowing me. It's so quiet. It's solitary confinement.

My only hope is His promise never to leave me nor forsake me. In my all-encompassing aloneness, I am tempted not to believe it. But the ache is so deep. You want to get lost in busyness, noise, and projects, but the motivation is not strong enough to move you. You already know the aloneness is still there in the busyness, the noise, and the work. The joy of companionship is missing wherever you go. Its absence aches behind your every smile. Where has my Love gone? He's gone to "the garden" of my soul to see if what He planted is growing.

He's gone to see if the lying dead face of aloneness will convince me I am alone. All my surroundings echo the silence of aloneness, and it pulls upon me. Her eyes lock into my gaze, and say without words, "I know what He has said, but what do you feel?" I feel alone. "What do you hear?" I hear nothing. "What do you see?" I see my four walls and me.

Aloneness is loud with want. In the silence, you are forced to feel the size of your want. It's bigger than you. You can't possibly wrap your arms around its enormity. Like the universe, you can't see the end of it, nor can you control it. All you can do is want. All you have is His word, but it doesn't change your experience. It just tells you the truth. It's as if that is all there is to your existence: want. You can't imagine there is anything big enough to fill it. I want to push it away with business, food, sleep, and accomplishment. I wish I could dig into the center of my being and pull it out of me. I imagine it would be like pulling out an infinity scarf to find out there is no end to it, and it's no trick. Every pull only proves there is no end to my want. She stares at you, reminding you how uneventful your beginning was, suggesting you are a fool to think your end will be any different.

It would be another ten months before I would meet Gary Elliot for the first time. What I don't have room to share is all the other promises God planted within those 25 years. If you read through Abraham's experience of hearing, waiting, and believing God, you'll see that every time Abraham wavered, God would visit him and add to the size of the promise. It went from a homeland to a son to countless descendants to a father of many nations. He pointed me to violets like He pointed Abraham to the stars and the sands of the sea to mark his memory with remembrances of what He said. He, too, waited 25 years to experience God's word becoming flesh in Issac. I've been known to say that everybody wants Abraham's faith, but nobody wants his journey.

I walked out to an empty old 1900s milk house on my property the morning of our wedding, where Gary had hidden my first birthday present. On my way, I caught myself walking over a single wild violet growing in my icy yard. It was November and bitter cold. Strangely enough, I was not surprised by it; I was warmed by it. Like Abraham's sand and stars, the violet was my relentless reminder of His promise. It was the last time God would give me "flowers" as a single woman to warm my heart and remind me of His words. Could our story get any more enchanting?

Yes, yes, it does.

Beale, Broadway, Bourbon, and back to Beale. The proverbial full circle to complete in my life had me wrapped in Gary's arms, prayer on our honeymoon and tucked inside in that red and white striped canopied cafe-styled blues joint. This was *that* place where one of my life's most pivoting and harrowing events was initiated. This was the place I first encountered the man who raped me. Surveying Beal Street with Gary that night for eats, I secretly wondered if I could ever trace the steps back there. It had been 26 years. No. I tried, but I couldn't. However, God could, and He did.

Before walking into that cafe, I stood on Beale Street that night without fear, regret, haunting shame, or phantom pains of what was once lost there. What had been meant for evil years ago turned into a goodness I had no capacity to imagine was possible at the time. Twenty-six years later, our steps so perfectly aligned without any foreknowledge or remembrance on my part. It was a divine alignment. I walked back into the "scene of the crime" from where my virtue was stolen and took a seat next to my husband of promise.

When I took Gary's hand, looked him in the eye, and said, "This is it; this is the place." I watched this man go from stunned to gallant without missing a beat. His first question was to ask if I was okay. I replied, "Yes. Strangely enough, yes. Actually, I can tell my healing is complete in me because there is no grief, anger, or trauma rising in me. I went looking for it; instead, I'm at total peace. I'm just kind of caught in unbelief." He began to thank God for my story, now our story. He thanked God for His redemption in my life, my daughter, and the gift I was to him now. He prayed for the salvation of the man who violated me. Unbelievable, he was just unbelievable.

Slowly, the bluesy tones lofting from the sunken stage in the next room cleared from being softened background music, insulating our encounter into a familiar song, "I needed the shelter of someone's arms / and there you were / I needed someone to understand my ups and downs / and there you were / with sweet love and devotion / deeply touching my emotion / I want to stop and thank you, baby / I wanna stop and thank you, baby; yes, I do / How sweet it is to be loved by you. Yes, God used a James Taylor song to add icing to one of the sweetest redemptive encounters of our lives together (How Sweet It Is James Taylor, Songwriters: Lamont Dozier / Brian Holland / Edward Jr. Holland.)

The last night of our honeymoon was one of the most profound experiences of both our lives. Memphis was our halfway stop between Illinois and New Orleans. Memphis, where my life's plans hit the proverbial sandstone wall. Memphis, where my innocence was raped from me. Memphis would now be where my redemption enjoyed its vengeance. I walked over to the cafe, the cafe that Gary had chosen on a "whim" and into a divine encounter waiting for us.

I was the girl who believed in destined romance. Twenty-six years ago, I was the girl sitting in this cafe/bar, determined to wait for destiny to line me up with my "prince charming" someday. I was the girl

261

who would not settle for less than something divine. It was as if Hell knew it, stuck out its foot, and tripped me, hoping I would fall into a future full of despair. It did not work. It backfired. I moved from violation to victory and sat next to the "prince charming" only "destiny" could line up. There I was redeemed, healed, full of God's joy and peace, hand in hand with my promised husband, sitting in the very room meant to end my dreams, giving thanks to God. What a divine setup! What the enemy meant for evil, God meant for good, and He took His sweet vengeance on our honeymoon to rub it in his face. I still can't get over it.

Early the next morning, before Gary woke, God's presence visited my spirit with an experience of His pleasure over us. He was so proud of us in that moment and with our chaste waiting for the one He wanted to reveal to us: me for Gary, Gary for me. It felt like God was experiencing the pleasure and honor only a Father can feel when His kids trust Him to the utmost as He joyfully celebrates the display of another defeated attempt to steal life. Not only was it sweet to be loved by Gary. It was sweet to be loved by God, and it was sweet for God to be loved back by us.

So, what did I do with this revelation? I cried. I cried hard. I was overwhelmed by the uphill distances we walked in Christ toward one another and the abounding grace God provided us to stay the course. I was overwhelmed with being someone who could give God such pleasure as He was allowing me to feel that morning. Who were we that He would even be mindful of us and that we could move the heart of God? Poor

Gary, we'd only been married six days before he had to wake up to a crying wife in his bed.

To this day, I have a calendar reminder on my phone for March 31st to celebrate my daughter's conception day. I have forgotten the pain of the violation to the point that I need a reminder that March 31st matters for a completely different reason, a redeeming reason. When you yield your life to Christ, His pleasure, and His plans, you will walk a very unusual path to healing, identity, and calling. He will not give you a map because you'd see too many reasons not to go with Him.

Our waiting for the one God would have for us was unusually long but uniquely designed to tell an unbelievable story of His faithfulness and His power residing in us to see it to its fulfillment. I said before that I never wanted an ordinary life. I wanted a life that could not be explained outside of the Holy Spirit. I got it, along with unending love, assurance, and peace from God that passes all understanding. These are the sure things, the eternal attributes I needed to wait well and now live well within the promise. I'll never be without them, come what may.

I wanted to be married at age 26. He never said no. He said, "Call upon Me, and I will answer you and show you great and mighty things, fenced in and hidden, which you do not know yet" (Jeremiah 33:3). With that, He changed me, filled me, and empowered me with His love. His love was needed first and foremost. Have you ever wanted to be so healed from your damage that you'd need to put a reminder in your phone that it ever happened? That kind of healing is possible. It was a walk of faith into a promise that was used to heal me, transform me, and eventually bless me beyond my imagination.

Gary and I were traveling back to Illinois a couple of weeks back. I asked him what he hoped you, our reader, would take away from our love story. He hopes you will come away confident, knowing God will provide a spouse who fits you just like He did for the first couple, Adam and Eve. God set a precedent in Genesis for you to trust in His providence and His provision to do for you what you could not do for yourself. This is the knowledge called faith, and it's the knowledge that makes you rest.

The American dating culture is full of striving, calloused hearts, and fainting wills, while the best Father you will ever have stands by waiting for you to R.S.V.P. on that invitation dropped in the Garden of Beginnings. In your pain, regret, and hopelessness, He is whispering over you, "Call upon Me. I will answer you. I am overflowing with things to show you, the things of mystery and intrigue you'll never know outside of knowing My love first and foremost."

And that is my hope. Through our love story, I hope you will see the best Father you will ever have, the most excellent Companion you will ever know, and the greatest Friend you'll ever need: God the Father, God the Son, and God the Holy Spirit. They are the three in one who complete you. They are the One who loved you first, Who will love you the most, and Who will be your unending resource to love others beyond what they deserve. They are the One Who knows your end from your beginning, every good work planted within your path, and They are the power to see you through to your hopes, dreams, and transformation.

If you believe Christ's death on the Cross paid for all your sins —past, present, and future—you are full of His very Spirit, which is an unending supply of love and power. You have been made perfect before Him and will spend the rest of your days discovering the new creation He has made you to be. It is no longer you who live, but your new life is about Christ living within you and from you to others.

I wish I had the imagination to write a love story like this. All I had was my obedience to the desires of His heart, which in turn became my desires, too. As Gary and I first grew in relationship with Him alone, His love and brilliant ways filled our lovesick hearts to overflow, where everything we were white-knuckling for ourselves lost its appeal. My words are weak in describing His love. Paul prays in Ephesians 3:18 that he would have the power to comprehend His love. Think about that. What kind of love is this that takes the power of His own Spirit to enable us to understand it?

It's too much.

We Christians are a family who believes in degrees of impossibility. We believe in His salvation from an eternal Hell without our help. We believe He forgives the unforgivable without our help. We even believe He'll save us a front-row parking spot at Walmart without our help. Why will most of us not believe He will give us the desires of our hearts in a husband or wife without our help?

God has helped Gary and I to know why: we don't believe we are worth the wait, nor do we believe there is anything worth waiting for in romance. Therefore, we don't wait and we go ahead helping ourselves in order to avoid confronting the deep, deep fear of our worthlessness. While we are busy striving to prove our worth, Perfect Love, who is a person, Christ Himself, stands by, waiting to cast out that fear through His own truth: while we were found worthless, He died to be with us once and for all (Romans 5:8 paraphrased). The truth about the value of anything is found in what someone is willing to pay for it. Perfect Love was given in order to have the opportunity to live in you and with you forever. The eternal truth is that you can never be more loved and worth it all than you are right now. Christ holds the only receipt in the shape of His cross, "For God has proved His love (to us) by giving us His greatest treasure, the gift of His Son (Perfect Love)..." It doesn't stop there, "... And since God freely offered Him up as the sacrifice (payment) for us all, He certainly won't withhold from us anything else He has to give." (Romans 8:32 TPT). See, not only are you worth waiting for, but so are the gifts He is preparing to give you, especially the gift of a spouse.

I pray the next time you see wild violets blooming in the Spring, you'll remember the promises of God over your own life, the good plans He had in mind for you while you were not yet born, still an unformed substance in your mother's womb. I also pray He walks you up to a violet in the snow to increase your enchantment in His profound faithfulness, proven in our story.

And as you wait for the words of God to become flesh in your life, Jesus is with you as you wait, as you doubt, as you mourn. He is near to the brokenhearted, an ever-present help in trouble. Even if you were never to set foot inside all the desires you desire, the companionship of Jesus along the way will be enough. He is your prize, your Shield and exceedingly great reward! No one can love you like He can—your Savior, your Creator, your Bridegroom. And no one can love Him back like you —His Beloved, His Friend, His Joy set before Him.

He is worthy of your trust and your relentless gaze. Don't look down at the faces of past defeats. They will try to seduce you into despair. "Be strong and courageous. Do not fear or be in dread of them, for it is the Lord your God who goes with you. He will not leave you or forsake you" (Deuteronomy 31:6).

Oh, and one last note: I finally got me some genuine Converse Chuck Taylors! They came with "the one" God had for me. My first official Chucks was Gary's first gift to me when we got engaged, and they have now kicked off into a whole collection... a love of good measure can be given to you too: pressed down, shaken together and running over poured into your lap. Father God's invitation is waiting for you: "Come, and I WILL make for you a suitable helper."

Gary & Kim Elliot are Co-Founders of God of the Romantic Presentations. Residing in Nashville, TN, they are passionate about seeing singles come to rest in God's design and providence concerning their desires for love and marriage. Their redemptive love story can not be told without pointing to God's greater story in her life: His salvation, companionship, and purpose.

Visit **godoftheromantic.com** to learn more.

For speaking requests email: **contact@godoftheromantic.com**

Books by Kim and Gary Elliot are available at Amazon and **godoftheromantic.com/books**:

God of the Romantic by Gary Elliot

Veiled Unto His Pleasure by Kim Elliot

Choosing Life After Rape by Kim Elliot

Violets in the Snow by Gary and Kim Elliot

Made in the USA
Columbia, SC
14 December 2024

48207687R00150